YOUR JOURNEY WITH JESUS

JumpStart
Volume One

Dr. Paul M. Reinhard

D1377233

Out of the Box Publishing
San Bernardino

COPYRIGHTS AND PERMISSIONS
By:

Dr. Paul M. Reinhard

THE BIRTH OF JUMPSTART:

You are holding a unique book in your hand. There is nothing else quite like it. Pastor Paul was sitting at Georges restaurant in Colton, CA. His friend Frank said to him, "So, what are you going to write?" Frank knew Paul had been thinking and praying about this question for many months. Paul was in the D. Min. Program at Golden Gate Seminary and was stewing on discipleship, leadership, and mentoring. Most churches do not have a solid mentoring track for new believers. It is a critical piece of the discipleship process. Paul thought and prayed about the topics and scriptures that helped him find Christ and grow in his faith. He thought of the random process he followed over a span of many years.

When Frank went to the counter for the food Paul took out a pen and an old fashioned yellow pad. He wrote. It began in the Garden, THE SEPARATION. Christ fixed it at the cross, THE SOLUTION. Our first step of obedience is baptism, THE BATH. When we come up out of the water we receive the Holy Spirit, THE POWER. If a believer is going to know and grow they need to study God's Word, THE SWORD. As you grow in faith prayer becomes essential, THE CONNECTION. At this point Frank came back with breakfast and Paul said, "Don't talk." Frank smiled and ate.

God calls all His children to serve, THE INVITATION. If you're going to have a job in the Body of Christ you need tools, THE EQUIPPING. If God gives us gifts we ought to use them, THE STEWARD. Jesus had a plan for reaching the world, THE MISSION. It is essential we do God's plan God's way, THE METHOD. If we are going to serve God and make disciples we should know how to behave, THE DO'S and THE DON'TS. God calls leaders, teachers, and mentors to a higher standard so it is essential to explore, THE CHARACTER. Believers must know what healthy church life looks like, THE BODY. Last but not least God's people need a Biblical foundation for large groups, small groups, and mentoring, THE MODEL.

Frank was finishing his breakfast and Paul's food was sitting there cold. The working outline for JumpStart had begun. An intense season of prayer and preparation was finally down on paper. Paul wrote the Sessions for JumpStart, preached them, and finally used them as the basis for his Doctoral Project: **TRAINING MENTORS TO UTILIZE THE JUMPSTART CURRICULUM AT NORTHPOINT CHRISTIAN FELLOWSHIP.**

Paul's prayer is for mentors, mentees, small groups, and churches to open their hearts to God and one another. To dig deeply into the precious Word of God. His prayer is that souls are saved, lives changed, faith increased, chains broken, disciples made, and awesome Kingdom leaders raised up. He knows this will take much more than JumpStart, but every journey must have a first step! New believers need a logical journey of spiritual discovery. We need roots before we can blossom. May God bless your journey!

WELCOME TO JUMPSTART
Your Journey with Jesus

How do you plug into a new Church?
How do you discover the essentials of the Christian faith?
How do you begin the process of preparing for Christian service and leadership?

You are about to begin a sixteen-week journey that will JumpStart your spiritual life. If you are new to the Christian faith, this is a great place to begin. You will cover the key basics. If you are new to church life this will give you a keen sense of God's mission and method. If you are ready to get involved in service or leadership this will call, challenge, and equip you to know, grow, and go. There is something for everyone.

You are on your way to experiencing sixteen exciting topics. Throughout the week you will read Scripture, answer reflection questions, and memorize key Scriptures. Then you will meet with your Mentor or small group to share what God has shown you. This is the time when iron sharpens iron. This is when you share, question, pray, cry, laugh, and grow. This is your special time to meet with God and people who love you.

As you begin the Jumpstart journey keep the ultimate goal in mind. I pray you are on your way to becoming a fully committed and activated SOUL WINNING DISCIPLE MAKING CHRIST FOLLOWER! I want to help you meet Christ, know Christ, grow in Christ, follow Christ, and serve Christ. As you submit to His Lordship He will reveal your spiritual gifts and calling within the Body of Christ and the world. Use those gifts to His glory.

It is my belief that Jesus Christ calls all His disciples to make disciples. Christ followers invite others to follow Christ. This amazing process is thousands of years old. God sends people into our life to encourage our spiritual growth and then uses us to help encourage others in their spiritual growth. The modern American church does worship and small groups well. I pray JumpStart fills the disciple making hole and lights a fire in all our hearts.

Along the way I will encourage you to connect with your local church Celebration and a Life Group. I believe we worship together in Celebration. We do life together in Life Group. We grow and go deeper in Mentoring. Do not get hung up on the names I call them. The important thing is the Scriptures we will study that ungird them.

I am excited God has brought us together. Each of us has sinned and been saved by grace. We are pilgrims on the Lord's highway. None of us has arrived yet. Nor do any of us have all the answers. Nevertheless, we should love wrestling with the questions. Thank you for the privilege of doing JumpStart with you. I love you and am already praying for you!

HOW TO BEGIN
JUMPSTART MENTOR TRAINING
AT YOUR CHURCH:

If you would like to schedule JumpStart
mentor training for your church or organization
please contact Pastor Paul.

Paul is also available for evangelism,
preaching, and small group training.

He Pastored NorthPoint Christian Fellowship
in San Bernardino, California for twenty-one years.

They survived and unified terrible division,
a name change, a change of constitution/by-laws,
a very expensive arson fire, and sanctuary rebuild,
bankrupt insurance company, capital funds campaign,
six years of setup and teardown at an Elks Lodge.

Paul loves to coach Pastors and Churches who are in the midst
of trials, transitions, and visioning their next season of ministry.

He can be encouraging, thought provoking, and annoying.
Ex-Green Beret Pastors tend to think that way!

Call/Text:
1-909-855-9695

Email:
PAULMREINHARD@GMAIL.COM

Jumpstart Journey Guide:

Introduction:

Each week we will introduce the Session and give you a sense of the topic you will cover. Jumpstart intends to help a seeker become a Christian, a Christian to become an active church member, and an active church member to become a SOUL WINNING DISCIPLE MAKING CHRIST FOLLOWER. It is my prayer this study is a key step on the path to raising up and equipping leaders to win cities for Jesus one person at a time.

Key Verse:

The Word of God is living and active. It is our sword. It has the power to rebuke, correct, educate, and train the aspiring servant of God. Each week you will spend time reading the Scriptures. The Sessions begin with a topic but grow out of the Word. Allow time to read the Word. Meditate on the Word. Reflect on the Word. Chew on the Word. As the Word of God penetrates your innermost being you will find your mind, and your spirit, beginning to change. The Word will turn you from the world, to Christ. It will cut your chains to the past and equip you for your amazing future.

Each week there will be a Key Verse for Memorization and Reflection. This verse will capture the heart of the Session. Spend time with the Key Verse each day. This will allow the theme of the week to work into your spirit and stir your thinking.

Lesson:

During the Lesson, you will examine Scriptures that unpack the week's topic. There will be some commentary, some sharing, and some stories. Mostly, there will be questions to guide you into the rich meaning of the Scriptures. These will not be exhaustive studies of the Scripture. That is a lifetime process. These are portions of the Scriptures many Christian leaders have found uniquely helpful in JUMPSTARTING their spiritual journeys. This may be review, or your introduction to a lifetime of exciting Bible study!

Conclusion:

Here you will find some closing and challenging thoughts. Our desire is for each Session to open your thinking to a key concept in your Christian faith. Over the weeks you will build upon what you have learned and go deeper in your understanding of what it means to live, serve, and minister as a Christian. Learning is the first step toward becoming which leads to doing. I want you being and doing for Jesus!

JumpStart Sessions Overview: Your Journey with Jesus
Volume One

1-1   The Separation   What did God create you to be and do?
What happened to mess it up?

2-6   The Solution   Adam and Eve lost it, but Jesus Christ got it all back.

3-13   The Bath   Taking a bath is part of cleaning up! Baptism is the public proclamation of your new life in Jesus Christ.

4-21   The Power   God has given you an amazing source of power, education, and comfort. Who is the Holy Spirit, and what part does He play in your life?

5-41   The Sword   Christians have enemies. You are a soldier in a battle. God gave you a very powerful weapon. Check out the sword of the spirit, which is the Word of God.

6-55   The Connection   Prayer was the original mobile phone. Our God never drops a call.

7-67   The Invitation   God has work for His children to do. Whom does He call? Whom does He use? What might God have for you?

8-77   The Equipping   You need tools for the job. God has given every one of His children an awesome spiritual gift, talent, and ability. What gifts can God give you to accomplish the ministry He has uniquely called you to do?

JumpStart Sessions Overview: Your Christian Discipleship Volume Two

9-1	The Steward	Because we are God's children, and because He has given us work to do, He will give us resources to use on His behalf. When we truly see ourselves as a pipeline from God to the world it will change how we see our time, talent, and treasure.
10-16	The Mission	God calls us to share His good news with the world. We begin that process with our OIKOS. [Our immediate circle of influence.] You already interact with these 8-15 people on a weekly basis. God wants to reach them through you.
11-29	The Method	Jesus called his followers disciples. He called His disciples to make disciples. We are in that ancient line. How do we pass it on?
12-41	The Do's	What are appropriate things for Christians to do?
13-55	The Don'ts	What does God ask Christians not to do?
14-68	The Character	Character is a key requirement for Christian leaders. What is God's standard for His leaders? What does a Godly leader look like? What will bad character cost us?
15-82	The Body	When you become a Christian God welcomes you into His family. How do we work together in His Body, the Church?
16-93	The Model	Your final JumpStart Session will examine the role of large groups, small groups, and mentoring in the Biblical story. Churches may call these parts of the ministry by different names. But most healthy growing ministries have all three.

Thank You:

I am reluctant to say thank you because so many people have helped me on my life journey thus far. I feel bad leaving anyone out. So, to all of you who have been part of my journey, please accept my humble thanks.

To my dear sweet wife Karen, I say a huge thank you. You have bounced from Tujunga, to Glendale, to Sunland, to Fresno, to N.J., and San Bernardino. You did piece work to help me in school and you have done everything to help me in ministry. When most women are winding down and preparing for retirement you allowed me to gear up and do a D. Min. JumpStart would not exist if not for your amazing willingness to persist with me. I love you, honor you, and thank you. The best is yet to come.

To my amazing God loving kids who left their Fresno friends. I will never forget the night you looked at me across the kitchen table and said, "If God is calling you to school in Philadelphia then you better go. And we will go too!" What more can a father ever desire? Your spouses and children love and serve Jesus. I am so proud of all of you!

To my mother, father, sister, and Glendale family I say thank you. You showed me how to be a family. Every birthday, Mother's Day, Father's Day, and holiday. You always showed me love and let me know that my place at the table was always open.

To Camp Fox, Mr. Stewart, the Fort Bragg Navigators, and Chaplain Stephenson I say thank you for telling me about Jesus. To Dr. David Brown, Dr. Howard Taylor, Dr. Bruce Baloian, and Dr. Ralph Neighbour, Jr. I thank you for your patience, persistence, and faith in a sometimes taxing and troublesome student. To Michael Weiss who just sent JumpStart to the Congo for a Swahili translation, what can I say? You are my brother. Thank you, Leslie, Darla, Traci, and John for proofing my mess.

To my NorthPoint family who helped me struggle through my D. Min., beta tested, proof read, and critiqued JumpStart, I love you and thank you all very much. Your willingness to push me on means more than words can express. Giving me wings was God's plan.

Last but surely not least is my Texas team of proofreaders, encouragers, questioners, and prayer warriors. Perry, Della, Pat, Stan, Frank, Darla, Traci, Karen, Teri and all your kids. I love you and am proud to be one of you, Paul Alton Sandifer.

And to all who will spend time with JumpStart, a Mentor, and God's Word I bless you. I pray God builds you up, sends you out, heals your heart, fills your mind, and uses you to His glory in new and amazing ways! May JumpStart be a mustard seed in the hand of God. In Jesus mighty name, AMEN!

JumpStart Session 1

"The Separation"

Introduction:

Welcome to your very first Session of JumpStart. You are about to discover the source of the terrible separation existing in our world today. Countries fight countries and people have conflicts with other people. There is a reason for all this distress. It begins with our separation from God.

Genesis 1-3 has two accounts of the creation story.
One paints the "Big Picture" while the other goes into more detail.
Read them together and let them paint one awesome picture.

Key Verse for Memorization and Reflection: Genesis 1:1 (NLT)
In the beginning, God created the heavens and the earth.

Lesson:

Genesis tells the story of a great creation. It also reveals a tragic fall. This fall resulted in a terrible separation. Elements of this separation are still at work in the world today. Examine these key ideas in today's topic and apply them to your life and relationships!

1.　　Read Genesis 1:1-31

A.　　What does God say about you in verse 31?

_____

　　　How does this make you feel?

_____

B.　　In verse 26 God said, "Let Us make mankind in Our image." This simple sentence is very important. God is part of the Us. The Spirit of God is part of the Us. Colossians 1:13-17 gives the identity of the third and final member of the Us. Who is it?

_____

_____

2.   You are important to God. What did He create you to do? Genesis 1:26B

_____

_____

Compare 2 Timothy 2:12   _____

3.   Read Genesis 2

A.   What did God tell Adam not to do?   Genesis 2:15-17

_____

_____

B.   If you were Adam, would you have obeyed?
        What do you think you would have done? Why?

_____

_____

4.   Read Genesis 3

A.   How did the serpent twist the Words of God when he tempted Adam and Eve in
        Genesis 3:1-6?

_____

5.   Three terrible things happened when Adam and Eve disobeyed God.
        What were they? Genesis 3:7

_____

_____

        What did they feel and do?   Genesis 3:10

_____

_____

        Have you ever had these feeling? Have you ever hidden from God?

_____

_____

```
REMEMBER:
SIN IS THE SOURCE OF SEPARATION
```

6.   When Adam and Eve disobeyed God they turned on one another.
          Read Genesis 3:11-13

A.   Who did Adam blame for his sin?

_____

B.   Who did Eve blame for her sin?

_____

C.   Have you ever denied responsibility for your own actions and pointed the finger
          at somebody else? How did it work out?

_____

_____

7.   When Adam and Eve disobeyed God there were eternal consequences.
          What were they? Genesis 3:22-24

_____

_____

Conclusion:

This week's Session reveals the historical roots of the separation between God, us, and others. Have you ever experienced the separating power of sin in your own life or in the lives of those around you? Think about family, work, sports, and even church.

_____

_____

_____

_____

_____

Prayer:

Lord: Please begin the process of healing any broken relationships I may have. Open the door to You and others. I understand this may be a scary journey. I might not even be ready for it. But I ask You to come into my life and have Your way. In Jesus Name, AMEN

JumpStart Mentoring 1
"The Separation"

Checking In:

Take some time to disconnect from the rush of the day. Take a deep breath and relax. Find out how your mentor/mentee is doing. Pray for one another. Ask the Holy Spirit to come, be your teacher, and guide your time together. REMEMBER: This is your time. Some days you may go deeply into the topic. Other days you may focus on the pressing issues of life. There may be mentoring Sessions where you move the lesson to next week and go for lunch, a swim, or a hike. Stay on track, but stop and smell the roses! Enjoy God and each other. I want this to be a precious and wonderful time each week.

Conversation Starters:

1. What part of creation amazes you the most?
    [Sky, ocean, animals, etc.]

    _____

    _____

2. How did the family you grew up in connect with God? Did they connect?

    _____

    _____

3. How did this family get along with one another? How connected or disconnected are they today?

    _____

    _____

4. Have you ever felt disconnected from God?

    _____

    _____

5. How is your relationship with God doing right now?

    _____

    _____

    _____

6. How do you normally deal with relationships? Do you tend to stay connected or do you tend to disconnect?

_____

_____

_____

_____

7. Is there an area of active disobedience that is currently separating you from God?

_____

_____

8. Are you in any strained or broken relationships that need healing?

_____

_____

OIKOS:

Each mentoring Session will include an OIKOS thought. These thoughts will turn your attention to those around you. OIKOS is the Greek word for household. In ancient times a household could be made up of parents, children, grandparents, aunts, uncles, brothers sisters, servants, or workers. Throughout JumpStart we will examine how God uses the concept of OIKOS in our lives and the building up of His church.

JumpStart Session 2
"The Solution"

Introduction:

In Session one we examined the source and tragic result of our Separation from God. This week we are going to examine the glorious Solution to this Separation. The subject of salvation fills countless books. Studies on the cross of Jesus Christ fill countless shelves. This Session will only scratch the surface of this magnificent and infinitely important topic! Enjoy.

Key Verses for Memorization and Reflection: 2 Corinthians 5:21 (NLT)
For God made Christ, who never sinned, to be the offering for our sin,
so that we could be made right with God through Christ.

Lesson:

If sin was the source of our Separation from God, then sacrifice is the Solution. Salvation is simple and profound. The smallest child can sense the call of God's Spirit and respond in simple faith by "Giving their heart to Jesus." Adults have fallen to their knees and accepted Christ while watching a game of professional football, after seeing a sign with John 3:16 displayed by a fan. However, starting your car with the turn of a key is profoundly different from understanding what is happening "under the hood." Genesis showed you how sin separates fallen people from a Holy God. You have probably heard that the work of Jesus Christ on the cross-paid the price to reconcile you with your Holy Heavenly Father. Today you are going to look "under the hood" and find out why the cross of Christ is so important, and what gave it such amazing power.

1.   Revisit Genesis 3:22-24: What dramatic action did God take to keep Adam and Eve from approaching the tree of life? What is the point of the symbolism for us?

_____

_____

_____

_____

2.	Romans 5:12-21 connects Adam to Christ. Read the verses very carefully. Compare what Adam lost in the garden, and what Christ won for you at the cross.

What happened when Adam sinned? What things were lost?

_____

_____

_____

_____

_____

What did Christ restore for you? Or, what happened when Jesus died upon the cross?

_____

_____

_____

_____

_____

_____

3.	Now we are going to visit the O.T. and see the history of the Cross of Christ! Egypt held Israel captive four hundred years until God sent them a deliverer. Some say Moses the deliverer was a "type" of Christ. That means his role as rescuer was an example of what Christ would do thousands of years later for us. Moses and Pharaoh locked horns in a spiritual battle for the freedom and future of God's children. We find the spiritual pinnacle of that battle in Exodus 12. Read the entire passage and allow the story to speak to you before you work on the questions.

A.	What happened to the lamb or goat in Exodus 12:6?

_____

B.	What happens to the blood in Exodus 12:7?

_____

C.	In Exodus 12:12 who is God fighting against?

_____

D. What happened, or did not happen, to the Jews who were under the blood? Exodus 12:13

_____

E. Take a quick look ahead to Hebrews 9:22. This is key to understanding the entire O.T. sacrificial system, the Cross of Christ, and your salvation. What must happen to wash away a sin?

_____

_____

4. We are about to invite you into one of the most challenging reading assignments in the entire JumpStart process. It is also one of the most important! Hebrews 9 and 10 give a N.T. explanation for the O.T. sacrificial system. Then it explains how the work of Jesus Christ paid the price for all times. Ask the Holy Spirit to be your teacher as you read Hebrews 9 and 10. These passages explain what happened at the cross. They connect the O.T. Jewish history with our N.T. Christian reality. You become part of an ancient tradition when you ask Jesus Christ to forgive your sins. Accept God's gracious gift through Jesus Christ our Lord.

A. In Hebrews 9:6-8 we read about the Most Holy Place. This represented the presence of God. It was as close as a human could get to the Holy One. Whom did God allow to go there?

_____

What did they do to enter there?

_____

B. How does Hebrews 9:11 describe Jesus Christ?

_____

_____

C. How did Jesus get into the Heavenly Most Holy Place? Hebrews 9:12

_____

_____

D. What did Jesus do for you in Hebrews 10:10?

_____

_____

_____

E.   Use your imagination. What picture do you get of Jesus in Hebrews 10:11-14?

_____

_____

5.   We must say one more thing about our Salvation at this point. There are several
     pointed and challenging verses toward the end of Hebrews 10. What do they say
     to you about God's will for your life? What warning do they speak to you?

A.   Hebrews 10:23-25

_____

B.   Hebrews 10:26-29

_____

C.   Hebrews 10:35-36

_____

D.   Hebrews 10:37-39

_____

_____

Conclusion:

A terrible Separation occurred in the Garden of Eden. Jesus Christ accomplished a
glorious and eternal Solution when He shed His blood upon the cross. He has made us
Holy and perfect before the Father. Now we are in the process of learning to live out
what He accomplished. This week's Session should give you some excellent material to
wrestle with when you meet with your mentor. If Hebrews was confusing for you, do not
worry. Bring your thoughts and questions to your mentor. You can work on it together!
Have a great week!

Questions/Comments/Notes:

_____

_____

_____

_____

_____

OK, I know there are artist types working through JumpStart.
All these words will drive you crazy!
So here is space for you to draw what salvation looks like to you.

Jumpstart Mentoring 2

"The Solution"

Checking In:

This week took a dive into the deep end of the pool. Many long-time Christians could not explain the teaching of Exodus 12 and Hebrews 9-10. Frankly, most discipleship systems skip them, or abbreviate them. We chose not to. It is too good, and too important. Do not feel bad if you felt like you were swimming in deep water this week! It will not get any deeper than this!

Conversation Starters:

1. How was your week? How are you doing? Is there anything special going on you should pray about before you finish today?

_____

_____

2. How was the lesson this week? Have you studied this material before? Was it new for you?

_____

_____

3. How does what happened to the Egyptians in Exodus 12 fit your understanding of God? Does it seem rough?

_____

_____

4. How does Hebrews 9:22 fit into the "world view" of modern America?

_____

_____

5. Review Session question 2. What did Adam lose, and what did Christ win back?

_____

_____

_____

What have you lost to sin? What has Christ given you back?

_____

_____

_____

_____

6.   Are you still living with the consequences of sin? This could be your sins, or
      the sins of somebody else.

_____

_____

7.   Are there things Christ needs to heal, forgive, or change in your life?

_____

_____

8.   What did the Hebrew 9 and 10 passages say to you?

_____

_____

9.   Go back to question 5 in the Session. What did these verses say to you?
      Did they scare you? Do they challenge you?   How?

_____

_____

OIKOS:

Scripture shows us God did not just save individuals. Often times he moved and saved
families, cities, and even countries. As you begin your JumpStart journey be aware of the
ways God is working in those around you. He wants your whole circle of influence.

Prayer Guide:

Take some time to thank God for saving you. Thank Jesus for His
obedience to God at the cross. If you have been taking His work on the
cross lightly, or living loosely, ask Him to rekindle your passion for His
presence, and His purpose for your life.

Jumpstart Session 3

"The Bath"

Introduction:

Bravo to you for working through last week's Session. I pray the Holy Spirit touched you through the amazing work of Christ upon the cross. Today we are going to look at the first act of obedience which follows our salvation. You are going to look at one of the most important, yet controversial, actions of our faith. You will be studying water baptism. We will affectionately call this experience a "Holy Bath." I am not aware of any Christian Churches which do not perform some kind of baptisms. The difference is some churches baptize babies while others baptize adults. Some sprinkle with a handful of water while others fill a tub and dunk you all the way under. As you wrestle with what the Word says about baptism, and my understanding of the Scriptures, I encourage you to be gentle and respectful of other people's traditions and experiences.

Key Bible Passages:
Romans 6:1-4, Acts 2:36-40, Matthew 3:4-17, Acts 8:26-38

Key Verse for Memorization and Reflection: Matthew 28:19 (NLT)
Therefore, go and make disciples of all the nations,
baptizing them in the name of the Father
and the Son and the Holy Spirit.

Lesson:

Salvation is a very personal and internal event. Christ gave His life for us and we give our life to Him. He died for us, and we commit to live for Him. Everybody has his or her own personal journey to Jesus.

Baptism is just the opposite. No matter how you came to the foot of the cross, you will publicly declare your allegiance to Christ in the same way millions have done before you! First, you will look at WHY we do this. Then you will look at HOW we do it. Lastly, we will examine the stories of some saints of old who have gone before you. Be open to the Word of God challenging your traditions. If God is calling you to take a step of trust and obedience I pray you are ready to take it. Especially if you are coming to Christ as an adult.

1. What is baptism?

A. Read Romans 6:1-4. When you are baptized, you act out the resurrection story of Jesus Christ. Three very important things happened to Jesus at the cross. When you join yourself with Jesus, you spiritually "re-enact" and follow Christ in these events. What are they?

     (1.) _____

     (2.) _____

     (3.) _____

B. As the Apostle Paul tells us...

> Just as Christ was raised from the dead
> by the glorious power of the Father,
> now we may live new lives.
> Romans 6:4 (NLT)

Paul said the same thing in Ephesians 1:19-20 (NLT)

> I also pray that you will understand the incredible greatness of God's power
> for us who believe him. This is the same mighty power that raised
> Christ from the dead and seated him in the place of honor
> at God's right hand in the heavenly realms.

We will study the Holy Spirit in a future Session. For now, rejoice in the fact the same power [Greek: *dunamis*] that raised Christ from the dead is at work within you now that you are His child.

How do you feel about the fact, God gives you the power to live a new life?

_____

_____

C. Galatians 3:26-27 gives us several truths about baptism. Which ones speak to you? Why?

_____

_____

D. In Matthew 3:4-6 we see John the Baptist preaching and baptizing. A key element must exist for a baptism to be real. What is it?

_____

_____

_____

E. In Acts 2 Simon Peter preached an awesome sermon in the power of the Holy Spirit. God launched the early church on that day. Read Acts 2:36-40. Pay special attention to verse 38. Peter gives us several things we must do. What are they?

1. _____

2. _____

3. _____

4. _____

Peter and Paul speak about the same promise. They declare the availability of the gift of the Holy Spirit. Paul calls it the same resurrection power which raised Christ from the dead. It is the power which allows us to live with and for Christ!

According to Peter, what group of people may receive this gift? [Verse 39]

_____

Remember:
Going to church does not make you a Christian
any more than going to McDonalds
makes you a Chicken Sandwich.
Baptism on the outside is meaningless unless
you have repented of your sins
and cried out to God on the inside!
In order for God to give you a new life
you must be ready to let go of your old life!

F. What two things happened for the 3,000 who believed in Christ when Peter preached on the Day of Pentecost? [Verse 41]

_____

_____

2.   Now we will look at the HOW of baptism. This special event should unite all Christians. Sadly, it often divides them. Some groups of believers baptize infants by sprinkling. Others only baptize by immersion or "going under the water." Some groups baptize children. Others wait until an "age of understanding." This next section will share my understanding of baptism. If you attend a church with a different understanding I pray you talk this through with your Mentor, small group leader, or Pastor. Then, do what you feel God and His Word are calling you to do.

As a pastor, I love to baptize people who have:

    (1.)   Heard and understood the gospel.
    (2.)   Repented of their sins and believed in Jesus Christ.
    (3.)   Desire to leave their old life behind.
    (4.)   Earnestly desire to be conformed to the image of Christ.
    (5.)   Are ready to publicly profess their commitment to Christ.
    (6.)   Understand the symbolic importance of this experience.

Thought:

We will never be perfect in this lifetime. So baptism is not for perfect people. Baptism is for people who want to profess their faith in Jesus Christ and take a public step of obedience. Do not let fear, guilt, or a misplaced sense of perfectionism keep you from taking this blessed step. We will never be worthy of baptism. It will always be God's gift of grace. We simply receive and respond. Your journey with Jesus will be made up of thousands of acts of faith and obedience. Baptism is just the first.

A.   Matthew 3:13-17 describes the baptism of Jesus. Examine verse 16 for clues about how Jesus was baptized. What did you find?

_____

_____

_____

B.   Acts 8:26-38 tells the story of Philip and the Ethiopian. This is an awesome story revealing some of the unique ways the Holy Spirit can work to bring someone to Jesus Christ. Enjoy the story. Then look at verses 38-39 for a hint about HOW Philip baptized the Ethiopian. What do you see?

_____

_____

C.   Look at the wonderful pattern in Acts 18:8 (NLT).

> Crispus, the leader of the synagogue,
> and everyone in his household believed in the Lord.
> Many others in Corinth also heard Paul,
> became believers, and were baptized.

People in Corinth heard Paul preach the gospel, they believed,
and went down into the waters of baptism.

Conclusion:

Colossians 2:12 (NLT) gives us a beautiful snapshot of the N.T. teaching on baptism.

> For you were buried with Christ when you were baptized.
> And with him you were raised to new life because you trusted
> the mighty power of God, who raised Christ from the dead.

Dietrich Bonhoeffer was a great German Pastor and teacher. Heinrich Himmler had him killed near the end of WWII for his part in a failed plot to assassinate Hitler. He is the source of one of my favorite quotes!

WHEN JESUS CHRIST CALLS A MAN
HE BIDS HIM COME AND DIE!

Baptism is the outward symbol of your inner decision to follow Jesus Christ to the cross, down into the grave, and upward to new life in God's Kingdom! When we go down into the waters of baptism we die to sin, self, and our old life. We arise a new creature in Christ endued with life giving power from on high through the infilling of God's Holy Spirit. Baptism is the public profession Christian's share by declaring to the world their desire to abide in Christ and join His Church!

There is a beautiful N.T. pattern. People heard the message. They believed the message. They received Jesus. Then they "went down into" the waters of baptism as a sign of their desire to follow Christ. Old things have truly passed away and you are new.

A Joyful Thought:

Just now, I finished using JumpStart to lead a baptism class with ten people new to church. They reminded me of something important us old pastors can forget. Baptism is fun, it is exciting, and it represents a glorious new beginning. It marks the end of what may have been a crazy season of somebody's life. Adults do not approach baptism in a casual manner. It is a very significant, and joyful, spiritual birthday.

It is life, and it has great emotional power. Good theology is important. But I pray God always reminds me of the overflowing joy and exuberance that accompanies baptism. In August of 2015 I had the privilege of helping baptize 1500 people on one day in Abidjan, Ivory Coast, Africa. It was necessary to monitor people's arms when they came up out of the water. They were so excited, dancing, jumping, leaping, and swinging about, that with ten of us in the baptismal at a time, someone could get knocked out. That is the glorious part of baptism I never want to lose.

I have come to the place where I ask the baptismal candidate who they desire to baptize them. This could be a pastor, their mentor, Life Group leader, or the person who brought them to Christ. It is exciting to teach somebody how to do a baptism. Where to stand, what to say, and what to do.

It is building a real sense of ownership into the SOUL WINNING DISCIPLE MAKING CHRIST FOLLOWING process. If my job as a pastor is to "Equip the saints for the work of their ministry," and I believe it is, then training others how to do a baptism is part of my job. (Ephesians 4:11-12) You will look deeper into the Biblical call God has given every believer in Session Seven, "The Invitation."

Jumpstart Mentoring 3
"The Bath"

Checking In:

By week three you should have some idea what to expect in your mentoring time. I hope God continually surprises you! My goal is for you to study the material on your own but process and apply it together. There is safety when you do theology in community. More than that, I am trusting God to show up and lead you into areas I have not even thought to ask about. Focus upon the Session. Yet, at the same time, be ever ready for God to raise an issue He wants you to explore. Trust God and your mentor.

Conversation Starters:

1. Begin by going over any parts of the lesson you really liked, or that caused you distress.

2. Share with your mentor about the life, death, burial, and resurrection of Jesus Christ. How is His life acted out when you go "down into the waters of baptism?"

3. Share the story of your baptism.
   Describe the place where your baptism occurred.

   Describe the method of your baptism.

   Were you sprinkled as a child, or an adult? Where you baptized "under the water?"

   Who baptized you?

4. What was the motive for your baptism? Was it out of tradition or expectation?

Was it a sincere spiritual experience?

_____

_____

5.   If you have not been baptized are you ready to follow Christ in baptism?

_____

_____

6.   What, if anything, is holding you back?

_____

_____

**If you are ready for baptism,
please let your Mentor, Shepherd, or Pastor know.
They would love to help you schedule this special event.**

OIKOS:

If God is calling you to be baptized it is the perfect time to invite your family, friends, coworkers, and neighbors to church. Baptism is a joyful public testimony of your commitment to follow Jesus. Work with your Pastor, Mentor, or small group leader to find the best method of inviting your OIKOS to celebrate your journey. It will be an amazing opportunity for them to hear about Jesus and reflect on their own spiritual journey. Do not assume your friends won't come, until you give them the chance. Ask them, and see what God is up to.

Prayer Guide:

Lord: Please open my eyes to the spiritual needs of those in my OIKOS. Show me how to invite them to come and celebrate my baptism. Draw them to Yourself so they can hear the preaching of Your Word, and believe. I pray you would lead my entire circle of influence into a personal relationship with You. Use me and this special time as a testimony to your saving power.   In Jesus name, AMEN

Jumpstart Session 4
"The Power

Introduction:
The Holy Spirit is the Third Person of the God Head. This means He is part of the trilogy we know as the Father, Son, and Holy Spirit. I find this idea of Trinity, or God Head, to be a baffling mystery. The Bible declares God is one! Yet there is a Father, Son and Holy Spirit. Many books exist on the subject. I just accept it while standing in complete awe! In this Session, we will look at 42 key verses that identify unique aspects of the Holy Spirit. Spend reflective time with the verses, and be amazed at the diversity and importance of the Holy Spirit. Allow one, two, or even three weeks for this Session. Do not rush. Enjoy!

Key Bible Passage:
In this Session I have implanted the verses for you. This will allow you maximum time in the Word with a minimum amount of page turning. We will also use the NASB for this Session. The New American Standard Bible is one of the most literal [word for word] translations. For this word-specific study I wanted to be as close to the original Greek as possible.

Key Verse for Memorization and Reflection: John 16:13 (NASB)
"But when He, the Spirit of truth, comes, He will guide you into all the truth;
for He will not speak on His own initiative, but whatever He hears,
He will speak; and He will disclose to you what is to come.

Lesson:
Long ago my first pastor told me, God the Father is the central character of the Old Testament. Jesus Christ is the centerpiece of the New Testament. The Holy Spirit is the power source for the church. He said that people love God because He is safely in heaven. They love Jesus because He lived 2,000 years ago. However, the Holy Spirit makes us nervous because He might show up and do something right here, right now. My prayer, as you begin this study, is the Holy Spirit will show up right here, right now. I pray He opens your eyes and reveals things you have never seen before! Do not be hesitant or afraid to explore the Holy Spirit. He is the wind of heaven. He is God. He is ready to blow new life into your spiritual journey. Discover Him for yourself in the Scriptures.

Special Instructions:

Each of the verses you are about to read reveals something unique about the person, work, or character of the Holy Spirit. Do not let this Session frustrate or overwhelm you. These are not trick questions. Some verses will say several things about the Holy Spirit. Some verses will say something and then apply it to the Holy Spirit. Be ready to think creatively and make the associations. If the verse seems unclear, try reading it in the translation you normally use. If things are still fuzzy check out the extra verses provided to help clarify what we are looking for from the verse. My desire is for you to discover the person, work, and character of the Holy Spirit for yourself, from the Scriptures. Find out who He is, what He did, and how He can work in your life today. Enjoy!

1.   Acts 10:38 (NASB) "You know of Jesus of Nazareth, how God anointed Him with the Holy Spirit and with power, and how He went about doing good, and healing all who were oppressed by the devil; for God was with Him.

1 John 2:27, 1 John 2:20 (NASB)

_____

_____

(Sample answer for #1: God anointed Jesus with the Holy Spirit, and power! Just allow the straightforward teaching about the Holy Spirit to surface.)

2.   Matthew 3:11 (NASB) "As for me, I baptize you with water for repentance, but He who is coming after me is mightier than I, and I am not fit to remove His sandals; He will baptize you with the Holy Spirit and fire.

Matthew 28:19, 1 Cor. 12:13, Acts 15:8, Acts 11:15-16, Acts 1:4-5, John 1:32-33, Luke 3:16

_____

_____

3.   Galatians 5:22-23 (NASB) But the fruit of the Spirit is love, joy, peace, patience, kindness, goodness, faithfulness, gentleness, self-control; against such things there is no law.

_____

_____

4.   Hebrews 10:15 (NASB)   And the Holy Spirit also bears witness to us.

_____

_____

5.   1 Chron. 12:18 (NASB) Then the Spirit came upon Amasai,
who was the chief of the thirty, and he said, "We are yours, O David,
And with you, O son of Jesse! Peace, peace to you, And peace to him who
helps you; Indeed, your God helps you!" Then David received them
and made them captains of the band.

Isaiah 59:21, Acts 20:28

_____

_____

6.   Matthew 12:31-32 (NASB)   "Therefore I say to you, any sin and
blasphemy shall be forgiven men, but blasphemy against the Spirit shall not
be forgiven. [32] "And whoever shall speak a word against the Son of Man,
it shall be forgiven him; but whoever shall speak against the Holy Spirit,
it shall not be forgiven him, either in this age, or in the age to come.

Psalm 51:11, Isaiah 63:10-11, Hebrews 10:29, Heb 6:4-6, 1 Thes. 4:8, 1
Thes. 5:19, Ephes. 4:30, Acts 7:51, Acts 5:3, Luke 12:10, Mark 3:29

_____

_____

7.   Acts 9:31 (NASB) So the church throughout all Judea and Galilee and
Samaria enjoyed peace, being built up; and, going on in the fear of the Lord
and in the comfort of the Holy Spirit, it continued to increase.

2 Cor 1:1-7, John 14:15-18, John 14:26, John 16:7

_____

_____

8.   Matthew 1:18 (NASB) Now the birth of Jesus Christ was as follows. When His mother Mary had been betrothed to Joseph, before they came together she was found to be with child by the Holy Spirit.

---

9.   Acts 1:8 (NASB) but you shall receive power when the Holy Spirit has come upon you; and you shall be My witnesses both in Jerusalem, and in all Judea and Samaria, and even to the remotest part of the earth.

1 John 5:8, 1 Thess. 1:5-6, 2 Cor. 6:6, 1 Cor. 12:3-4,
Acts 5:32, John 15:26

---

10.   Acts 13:52 (NASB) And the disciples were continually filled with joy and with the Holy Spirit.

Luke 1:41, Ephes. 5:18, Acts 13:9, Acts 11:23-24, Acts 9:17, Acts 7:55, Acts 4:31, Acts 4:8, Acts 2:3-4, Luke 4:1, Luke 1:67, Luke 1:15

---

11.   Hebrews 2:4 (NASB) God also bearing witness with them, both by signs and wonders and by various miracles and by gifts of the Holy Spirit according to His own will.

1 Cor. 12:11, 1 Cor. 12:7, 1 Peter 4:10-11, Romans 12:4-8

---

12.   Romans 15:13 (NASB) Now may the God of hope fill you with all joy and peace in believing, that you may abound in hope by the power of the Holy Spirit.

Clare Booth wrote,
"There are no hopeless situations;
there are only men who have grown hopeless about them."

Psa 125:1-3, Psa 33:18-20, 1 Pet 1:13, 1 Pet 1:3-5, Heb 10:23

_____

_____

_____

Reflection:
Is there an area in your life at this time where you need some hope?

_____

_____

13.   John 6:63 (NASB) It is the Spirit who gives life; the flesh profits nothing; the words that I have spoken to you are spirit and are life.

Galatians 5:25, Romans 8:11

_____

_____

_____

_____

Being Consistent:
The human body is a most remarkable machine.
It can maintain a constant temperature of 98.6 degrees no matter
what the weather is outside. Whether a man is at the Arctic Circle or the equator,
his body temperature is about the same.
There is an inner mechanism that makes the difference.
The Holy Spirit dwells within the Christian to achieve this kind of stabilization
in terms of spiritual health. Whether we face good times or bad,
whether we are tempted or receiving spiritual nourishment,
the Holy Spirit keeps us stable within.
Robert Shannon

14.   Romans 5:5 (NASB) and hope does not disappoint,
because the love of God has been poured out within our hearts
through the Holy Spirit who was given to us.

Col. 1:8

_____

_____

Love is, and isn't, Power:
Of all powers, love is the most powerful and the most powerless.
It is the most powerful because it alone can conquer that final
and most impregnable stronghold which is the human heart.
It is the most powerless because it can do nothing except by consent.
-- Frederick Buechner

Love for Enemies:
Agape love is the love of T. E. McCully, father of Ed McCully,
one of the missionaries slain by Auca Indians in Ecuador,
who one night shortly after that experience prayed,
"Lord, let me live long enough to see those fellows saved who killed our boys
that I may throw my arms around them and tell them I love them
because they love my Christ." That is love of the highest kind.
Author Unknown

Love is a Choice:
Always, love is a choice.
You come up against scores of opportunities every day to love or not to love.
You encounter hundreds of small chances to please your friends,
delight your Lord and encourage your family.
That's why love and obedience are intimately linked—
you can't have one without the other.
-- Joni Eareckson Tada,

Love is God's:
In the French revolution, a young man was condemned
to the guillotine and shut up in one of the prisons.
He was greatly loved by many,
but there was someone who loved him more than all the others put together.
That one was his own father, and the love he bore his son was proved in this way:
when the lists were called, the father-- whose name was exactly the same
as the son's--answered to the name,
and the father rode in the gloomy tumbrel out to the place of execution,
and his head rolled beneath the axe instead of his son's,
a victim to mighty love.
See here an image of the love of Christ to sinners.
For thus Jesus died for the ungodly.
-- Charles Haddon Spurgeon

Reflection:

Is there a difficult area of your life where God is calling you to offer agape love to someone? Have you a sense of what God is calling you to do? Are you willing?

_____

_____

15.   Mark 13:11 (NASB) "And when they arrest you and deliver you up, do not be anxious beforehand about what you are to say, but say whatever is given you in that hour; for it is not you who speak, but it is the Holy Spirit.

Mark 12:36, 2 Pet 1:20-21

_____

_____

16.   Romans 8:26 (NASB) 26 In the same way the Spirit also helps our weakness; for we do not know how to pray as we should, but the Spirit Himself intercedes for us with groanings too deep for words;

Jude 1:19-20, Ephesians 2:18, Romans 15:30,
Romans 8:26, Ephesians 6:18

_____

_____

17.   Luke 10:21 (NASB) At that very time He rejoiced greatly in the Holy Spirit, and said, "I praise You, O Father, Lord of heaven and earth, that You have hidden these things from *the* wise and intelligent and have revealed them to infants. Yes, Father, for this way was well-pleasing in Your sight.

_____

_____

Comment:

The word "revealed" in the passage above is *apokalupto* in the Greek N.T. It has the word picture of "pulling back or taking off the covers." Throughout the Bible we see the Holy Spirit working in our lives to "pull off the covers" we often use to hide ourselves from Him. Have you ever had a wrestling match with somebody trying to pull the covers off you? Do you ever wrestle with God about things He is trying to uncover?

Thought:

Imagine a small child in a lightning storm. The thunder is clapping and the lightning is shooting across the sky. Many children hide under the covers to protect themselves from the experience of the storm. Other children slip out of bed, go to the window, open the shutters, open the window, and peer intently into the glory of the night sky!

Question:

Do you *apokalupto* when you come to God in prayer or worship? Do you throw off the covers? Do you open up and expose all that you may have hidden? It is not always easy.

Challenge:

What a great image! Jesus was celebrating a holy moment with His disciples and His Heavenly Father. Jesus pulled back the covers in the power of the Holy Ghost. He pealed them back. He opened everything up, reached out, and touched God with nothing between them. He did it in the power and presence of the Holy Ghost. May Jesus ever be our model. May we forever throw off the covers in our worship of the Almighty. As we take this journey let us trust the Holy Spirit to lead us into God's presence and to keep us safe while we are with Him. He will never act contrary to our own best good!

Is there a special area where God is calling you to trust Him right now?

_____

_____

18.　　1 Cor. 6:15-20 (NLT) Don't you realize that your bodies are actually
parts of Christ? Should a man take his body, which belongs to Christ,
and join it to a prostitute? Never! And don't you know that if a man joins
himself to a prostitute, he becomes one body with her?
For the Scriptures say, "The two are united into one." But the person who
is joined to the Lord becomes one spirit with him.

Run away from sexual sin! No other sin so clearly affects the body as
this one does. For sexual immorality is a sin against your own body.
Or don't you know that your body is the temple of the Holy Spirit, who lives
in you and was given to you by God? You do not belong to yourself,
for God bought you with a high price.
So you must honor God with your body.

James 4:1-10

_____

_____

_____

19.　　Luke 3:22 (NASB) and the Holy Spirit descended upon Him
in bodily form like a dove, and a voice came out of heaven,
"Thou art My beloved Son, in Thee I am well-pleased."

_____

_____

20.　　John 16:7 (NASB) "But I tell you the truth, it is to your advantage
that I go away; for if I do not go away, the Helper shall not come to you;
but if I go, I will send Him to you.

_____

_____

21.   Acts 2:17-18 (NASB) 'And it shall be in the last days,' God says, 'That I will pour forth of My Spirit UPON ALL MANKIND; And your sons and your daughters shall prophesy, And your young men shall see visions, And your old men shall dream dreams; Even upon My bondslaves, both men and women, I will in those days pour forth of My Spirit And they shall prophesy.

Acts 2:33

_____

_____

22.   Acts 6:3, 5 (NASB) "But select from among you, brethren, seven men of good reputation, full of the Spirit and of wisdom, whom we may put in charge of this task. And the statement found approval with the whole congregation; and they chose Stephen, a man full of faith and of the Holy Spirit, and Philip, Prochorus, Nicanor, Timon, Parmenas and Nicolas, a proselyte from Antioch.

_____

_____

23.   1 John 4:13 (NASB) By this we know that we abide in Him and He in us, because He has given us of His Spirit.

1 John 3:24, Ephesians 1:13-14, 2 Cor. 5:5, 2 Cor. 1:22, Romans 8:16, Romans 8:23, John 7:39

_____

_____

24.   Ephes. 3:16 (NASB) that He would grant you, according to the riches of His glory, to be strengthened with power through His Spirit in the inner man;

2 Tim. 1:14, 2 Tim. 1:7, Acts 1:8, Luke 24:49, Luke 4:14

_____

_____

25.   Romans 1:3-4 (NASB) concerning His Son, who was born of a descendant of David according to the flesh, who was declared the Son of God with power by the resurrection from the dead, according to the Spirit of holiness, Jesus Christ our Lord.

_____

_____

26.   Romans 9:1 (NASB) I am telling the truth in Christ, I am not lying, my conscience bearing me witness in the Holy Spirit.

_____

_____

27.   John 14:26 (NASB) "But the Helper, the Holy Spirit, whom the Father will send in My name, He will teach you all things, and bring to your remembrance all that I said to you.

1 John 2:27, Luke 12:12

_____

_____

28.   Matthew 4:1 (NASB)   Then Jesus was led up by the Spirit into the wilderness to be tempted by the devil.

Acts 19:21, Acts 16:6, Acts 15:27-28, Acts 13:4, Acts 13:2, Acts 1:1-2, Luke 4:1, Mark 1:12

_____

_____

29.   Philip. 1:19 (NASB) For I know that this shall turn out for my deliverance through your prayers and the provision of the Spirit of Jesus Christ.

_____

_____

30.   1 Peter 1:12 (NASB) It was revealed to them that they were not serving themselves, but you, in these things which now have been announced to you through those who preached the gospel to you by the Holy Spirit sent from heaven-- things into which angels long to look.

1 Cor. 2:4 (NASB) And my message and my preaching were not in persuasive words of wisdom, but in demonstration of the Spirit and of power.

_____

_____

31.   2 Peter 1:20-21 (NASB)   But know this first of all, that no prophecy of Scripture is a matter of one's own interpretation, for no prophecy was ever made by an act of human will, but men moved by the Holy Spirit spoke from God.

Acts 21:11, Acts 21:4, Acts 20:22-23, Acts 11:28

_____

_____

32.   Ephesians 3:4-5 (NASB) By referring to this, when you read you can understand my insight into the mystery of Christ, which in other generations was not made known to the sons of men, as it has now been revealed to His holy apostles and prophets in the Spirit;

Hebrews 9:8

_____

_____

33.   Romans 14:17 (NASB)   for the kingdom of God is not eating and drinking, but righteousness and peace and joy in the Holy Spirit.

_____

_____

34.   **Galatians 3:5 (NLT)**
I ask you again, does God give you the Holy Spirit
and work miracles among you because you obey the law? Of course not!
It is because you believe the message you heard about Christ.

Romans 15:19

_____

_____

35.   Titus 3:5-6 (NASB) He saved us, not on the basis of deeds which we
have done in righteousness, but according to His mercy,
by the washing of regeneration and renewing by the Holy Spirit,
whom He poured out upon us richly through Jesus Christ our Savior.

_____

_____

36.   Luke 2:25-27 (NASB) And behold, there was a man in Jerusalem
whose name was Simeon; and this man was righteous and devout,
looking for the consolation of Israel; and the Holy Spirit was upon him.
And it had been revealed to him by the Holy Spirit
that he would not see death before he had seen the Lord's Christ.
And he came in the Spirit into the temple; and when the parents brought
in the child Jesus, to carry out for Him the custom of the Law,

1 Cor. 2:13-14

_____

_____

37.   2 Thes. 2:13 (NASB) But we should always give thanks to God
for you, brethren beloved by the Lord, because God has chosen you
from the beginning for salvation through sanctification
by the Spirit and faith in the truth.

Romans 15:16, 1 Peter 1:2

_____

_____

38.   Acts 8:29 (NASB) And the Spirit said to Philip,
"Go up and join this chariot."

Acts 11:12 And the Spirit told me to go with them without misgivings. And these six brethren also went with me, and we entered the man's house.

Hebrews 3:7, 1 Tim. 4:1, Matthew 22:43, Acts 28:25, Acts 10:19, Acts 4:25, Acts 1:16, John16:13

---

39.   Romans 8:4-6 (NASB) ...who do not walk according to the flesh, but according to the Spirit. For those who are according to the flesh set their minds on the things of the flesh, but those who are according to the Spirit, the things of the Spirit. For the mind set on the flesh is death, but the mind set on the Spirit is life and peace,

Galatians 6:8 (NASB) For the one who sows to his own flesh shall from the flesh reap corruption, but the one who sows to the Spirit shall from the Spirit reap eternal life.

Galatians 5:16-18, Romans 8:13, Romans 8:2, John 3:6

Human nature is not just frail and weak; human nature is also twisted and tangled.
Human perspectives, human understanding, and human efforts
are actually hostile to the perspectives, and understanding, and the plan of God.
We are morally inadequate, and we are driven toward rebellion.
-Lawrence O. Richards

Question for reflection:

Have the verses in #39 and the above quote by Lawrence O. Richards ever been true in your life? Think about the work that the Holy Spirit desires to do in and through you.

On a day-to-day basis do you feed the flesh or the spirit?
Do you have any habits or associations that must go
in order for the Holy Spirit to freely and fully lead you?

_____

_____

Thought:

What does it mean that the Holy Spirit spoke?
Was it a feeling? Was it a literal voice?
Was it a supernatural quickening of normal mortal thoughts?
Was it a push, a nudge, or a hunch?

However it happened, it is obvious the Holy Spirit did speak to the kings, prophets, and apostles. Jesus also promised He would speak to us! So, if I completely understand Him or not, the desire of my heart is for the Holy Spirit to come and speak to me. My desire is to learn how to listen for the voice of God through His Holy Spirit.

Time is involved! Listening is involved!
God's Word and God's people are absolutely involved!
This is a problem for many of us in this day and age.
We are bombarded by cell phones, computers, TV, and tablet.
We tend to run like chickens with our heads cut off.
Especially if we live in an urban or suburban setting.
Busy Busy Busy, Hurry Hurry Hurry, and Work Work Work!

The question becomes:
How do we slow down?
How do we pay attention to God?
How do we learn to listen and respond to the still small voice?

How do we stop our own running, striving, trying, and worrying
so we can receive what the King of Kings has offered to give us?

God said through the prophet Jeremiah,
"Call to me and I will answer you and tell
you great and unsearchable things you do not know."
(Jeremiah 33:3 NIV)

**Ask God to still your heart, quiet your mind, connect you,
and speak to you about the things you need to know.
Take the time to wait on God!**

Take the subtle messages seriously. If I hear something once. OK. If I hear the same thing twice I pay attention. However, if I hear the same thing three times within a short period of time from people or sources I trust I really pay attention and assume God is speaking to me. Then I check the message with the Scriptures and some trusted Christian friends. If everything lines up. I need to presume God is speaking and prepare to respond.

Is there something you believe God has been speaking or revealing to you recently?

_____

_____

_____

_____

40.   Ephes. 4:3 (NASB) being diligent to preserve the unity of the Spirit
in the bond of peace.

_____

_____

_____

41.   John 14:16-17 (NASB) "And I will ask the Father, and He will give
you another Helper, that He may be with you forever;
that is the Spirit of truth, whom the world cannot receive,
because it does not behold Him or know Him, but you know Him
because He abides with you, and will be in you.

_____

_____

42.   Acts 10:44-45 (NASB) While Peter was still speaking these words,
the Holy Spirit fell upon all those who were listening to the message.
And all the circumcised believers who had come with Peter were amazed,
because the gift of the Holy Spirit had been poured out
upon the Gentiles also.

Acts 2:38 (NASB)   And Peter said to them, "Repent,
and let each of you be baptized in the name of Jesus Christ for the
forgiveness of your sins; and you shall receive the gift of the Holy Spirit

John 20:22 (NASB)   And when He [Jesus] had said this,
He breathed on them, and said to them, "Receive the Holy Spirit.

Luke 11:13 (NASB)   "If you then, being evil,
know how to give good gifts to your children, how much more shall your
heavenly Father give the Holy Spirit to those who ask Him?"
Galatians 3:14, Galatians 3:2, Acts 19:6, Mark 1:10, Acts 19:2,
Acts 10:47, Acts   8:15-19

_____
_____
_____

**Artists and Doodlers,
draw the Holy Spirit at work in your life!**

Jumpstart Mentoring 4

"The Power"

Checking In:

You have now reflected on 42 key characteristics of the Holy Spirit. I pray your understanding of who the Holy Spirit is and what He does has grown. More than that, my prayer is you have sensed the Holy Spirit working actively in your day-to-day life. The goal is to know Him, not just to know about Him. Share the new insights you gained about the Holy spirit. Engage what He might be leading you to do in specific areas of your life. Take a chance.

Conversation Starters:

1. Begin by sharing any general thoughts or impressions you had during this week or weeks study. Yes, I know it was a long Session with lots of verses. LOL

_____

_____

2. Did anything special, unique, or supernatural occur for you during your studies?

_____

_____

3. Have you ever had any supernatural and/or unexplainable encounters with the Holy Spirit?

_____

_____

4. Share your thoughts on love. [Q. 14]

_____

_____

5. Share your thoughts on trust. [Q. 17]

_____

_____

6. Is there something you feel God has impressed upon you this week? [Q. 38]

_____

_____

7.   The spirit and the flesh are in constant conflict with our culture, and our souls. Share your thoughts and any challenges God has given you. [Q. 39]

_____

_____

8.   How can you walk in a closer daily relationship with the Holy Spirit?

_____

_____

Remember:

The Holy Spirit has an amazing array of communication techniques. He has manifested tremendous resourcefulness throughout history. If He has something for you, your group, church, or ministry He is well able to provide it. The Holy Spirit does not need us to whip Him up, get Him started, or help Him along. He needs us in an obedient, worshipful, and receptive posture. Be attentive and available. Not crazy, neurotic, or compulsive.

1 Samuel 3:7-9 (NLT)
Samuel did not yet know the LORD because he
had never had a message from the LORD before.
So the LORD called a third time, and once more Samuel got up
and went to Eli. "Here I am. Did you call me?"
Then Eli realized it was the LORD who was calling the boy.
So he said to Samuel, "Go and lie down again, and if someone calls again, say,
'Speak, LORD, your servant is listening.'" So Samuel went back to bed.

OIKOS:

This week you have seen the amazing diversity with which the Holy Spirit speaks, moves, and ministers in the lives of people. As you continue to study God's Word, pray, and share with your Mentor expect God to be at work in those around you. Remember that God saves families, cities, and even countries. He is at work within you and will use you as His witness with those special people He has strategically placed around you. Continue to look for His work in your OIKOS. Be ready when He prompts you. Until then be like Samuel, "Relax and go back to bed."

Prayer Guide:

Dear God:
Please forgive our sins in the name of Jesus!
Baptize us in your Holy Spirit!
Overcome the works of our flesh, our sin, and the devil!

Fill us with your spirit.
Be our teacher, our guide, our strength,
our wisdom, and our provision.

Let us do ministry.
Let us bear much good fruit.
Let us use the gifts you have given us.
Lead us, guide us, and protect us.

Fill us up with all the fullness of your presence
so we might by your agents of righteousness in this world!

Thank you, God, for the promise of your Spirit.
You, living in us is a concept we barely understand.
It is surely the journey we desire to be on!

Put evil far from us.
Consume us and have your way with us!

Conform us to the image of your precious Son
and to all your purposes for us in the world!

In Jesus name, Amen

Jumpstart Session 5
"The Sword"

Introduction:

If you search the phrase "Word of God" in the NASB Bible translation you will find 486 verses. If you search the "Word of the Lord" you will find 2,630 hits. If you add words like "Scripture, prophecy, revelation, study, meditate, God's law, or commands" you will find thousands more. The sixty-six books of the Old and New Testament are the written record of God's plan for His people. The Bible, more than any other source, teaches us what we need to know for life in this world and for the glories of heaven which are to come. In this Session we will allow the Scriptures to reveal their source, authority, and purpose in the life of both believers and unbelievers. This Session will introduce a topic worthy of a lifetime of diligent study.   Enjoy!

Key Verses for Memorization and Reflection: Ephesians 6:17 (NLT)
Put on salvation as your helmet, and take the sword of the Spirit,
which is the word of God.

Lesson:

My prayer is the Scriptures you are about to study will both challenge and encourage you. God's written Word is His primary method of communicating with His children. It is the foundation. It is the "Final Word." Today's Scriptures are verses that have challenged and directed me as I have lived and grown in my faith. I pray they will work deeply into your soul and bear amazing fruit in your life!

Preface:

I love watching hungry babies. They wiggle, grunt, snort, cry, and demand a feeding. Once a baby has found their target everything changes. They suck and nuzzle until they are full and contented. The writers of Scripture used this timeless illustration to teach us a great spiritual truth. It is proper and good for babies to be fed by others. As they grow up it is normal for them to begin feeding themselves. Healthy adults feed themselves and often become responsible for the feeding of others. It is the normal progression of life.

1 Peter 2:2-3 (NLT)
Like newborn babies, you must crave pure spiritual milk
so that you will grow into a full experience of salvation.
Cry out for this nourishment,
now that you have had a taste of the Lord's kindness.

1 Corinthians 3:1-3A (NLT)
Dear brothers and sisters, when I was with you
I couldn't talk to you as I would to spiritual people.
I had to talk as though you belonged to this world
or as though you were infants in the Christian life.
I had to feed you with milk, not with solid food,
because you weren't ready for anything stronger.
And you still aren't ready,
for you are still controlled by your sinful nature.

Hebrews 5:11-14 (NLT)
There is much more we would like to say about this,
but it is difficult to explain,
especially since you are spiritually dull and don't seem to listen.
You have been believers so long now that you ought to be teaching others.
Instead, you need someone to teach you again
the basic things about God's word.
You are like babies who need milk and cannot eat solid food.
For someone who lives on milk is still an infant
and doesn't know how to do what is right.
Solid food is for those who are mature,
who through training have the skill to recognize
the difference between right and wrong.

Isn't it amazing that three different authors in three different N.T. books tell us almost exactly the same thing. Nursing spiritual babies are awesome. Nursing spiritual teenagers are embarrassing. Nursing, milk drinking, long time Christian adults are just plain wrong! If you have been a Christian for a long time and still feel like a nursing baby, relax. The fact that you are doing JumpStart tells me you are ready to know, grow, and go. Praise God! I am so glad you are here and can't wait to see what God has for you. Seriously, it is never too late to dig into God's Word. Look to the future, not the past.

Question:

Which best describes your current spiritual age and relationship with the Word of God? Keep in mind, this has nothing to do with how old you are or how long you have been a believer. Be honest. This is just between you, God, and your Mentor if you share it.

A.   I am a hungry spiritual baby. I am eager for someone to feed me God's Word.

B.   I am growing and becoming a self-feeder on the milk of the Word.

C.   I am regularly self-feeding on solid spiritual food.

D.   I am hungry for spiritual food and desire to share what I learn with others.

E.   I might be on the verge of spiritual starvation.

1.   According to 2 Peter 1:20-21 and 2 Timothy 3:16 who is the authority behind the written Word?

_____

2.   Hebrews 4:12-13 lists several attributes of the Word. It also gives us a purpose for the word.

    A.   List the attributes:

_____

_____

_____

    B.   Find the purpose:

_____

_____

_____

WARNING:
This is a Really Gross but Pretty Good Example

As Pastor Paul was mentoring Ron Lee they began to dig deeply into Hebrews 4:12-13. They considered how, when you clean a fish, you hold it in your hand, roll it over onto its back, and insert your fillet knife in the lower region of its belly. You press down until the knife breaks through and penetrates the outer layer of skin.

You keep cutting upward until the entire belly of the fish opens wide. Then you can reach your hand inside and scoop out all of the guts and parts. You run the tip of your middle finger down the spine of the fish and separate the membrane and blood from the bone. You dig around with your hand until the inside of the fish is clean, the gross parts are gone, and it is ready to cook.

This is a graphic picture of God at work inside of us. He uses His Word in the hand of His Spirit to open us up so He can scoop out all the junk we have stored up inside. A well-cleaned fish is ready to fry and eat. A sanctified Christian is ready to serve. Commit to Christ and invite Him to send the Holy Spirit to apply the Word to your heart! It might hurt a little in the cleaning process but the end result is worth it. Just don't wiggle out of the Masters hand while He does His healing work in your heart!

I warned you it was a gross example!
But it's the truth!

3.   Close your eyes and spend time evaluating your attitude toward God and His Word in your life. Are you ready to allow the truth and teaching of God's Word to impact and address every facet of your life and character? Are you ready for the Spirit of God to use the Word of God to do spiritual surgery on your heart, mind, and soul? Have you submitted your heart and mind to the transforming work of God? If not, why not? What is holding you back? Give God permission right now to continue His work.

_____

_____

_____

4.   The Apostle Paul was a spiritual father to young Timothy. In 2 Timothy 3:10-17 we hear Paul's powerful and impassioned testimony and plea. Paul is pouring his heart out to young Timothy. He is declaring the lifestyle of God's servant, the cost of obedience, and the power God has given us in His Most Holy Word! Embrace Paul's challenge as you examine this powerful passage!

> A.   ¹⁰But you, Timothy, certainly know what I teach,
> and how I live, and what my purpose in life is.
> You know my faith, my patience, my love, and my endurance.

Does what you believe in your mind and say with your mouth about being a Christian match the life you are actually living and the things you are really doing? Does your life purpose align with the plan of God? Are you living on God's agenda or your own? Can you speak boldly into the life of a young believer like Paul did?

_____

_____

_____

> B.   ¹¹You know how much persecution and suffering I have endured.
> You know all about how I was persecuted in Antioch, Iconium,
> and Lystra—but the Lord rescued me from all of it.
> Yes, and everyone who wants to live a godly life
> in Christ Jesus will suffer persecution.

Can you think of situations in your life where putting the Word of God into practice might bring conflict or distress? Are you ready to deal with the changes total obedience to Christ might bring? Remember: It will impact those around you.

_____

_____

_____

C. ¹³But evil people and impostors will flourish.
They will deceive others and will themselves be deceived.
But you must remain faithful to the things you have been taught.
You know they are true, for you know you can trust those who taught you.

Are the spiritual leaders you follow committed to seeking and obeying the truth of God's Word?

_____

_____

D. ¹⁵You have been taught the holy Scriptures from childhood,
and they have given you the wisdom to receive the salvation
that comes by trusting in Christ Jesus.

What implication does verse 15 have for the children in your church?
Are you committed to teaching and winning the next generation for Christ?

_____

_____

E. ¹⁶All Scripture is inspired by God and is useful to teach us
what is true and to make us realize what is wrong in our lives.
It corrects us when we are wrong and teaches us to do what is right.

The Apostle gives us four powerful declarations about what the Word will accomplish in our lives. Identify the four things.

1. _____

2. _____

3. _____

4. _____

Are you seeking this instructional interaction with God's Word? Are you ready to be taught, convicted, informed, and transformed? God invites us into this humble and submitted relationship to Him through His Word! Is there anything holding you back?

_____

_____

_____

Reflection:

There is a point in your spiritual journey when the Word of God begins to speak into your life. The Spirit might apply the Word to your character, moods, marriage, temperament, job, habits, friends, family, drugs, alcohol, pornography, etc. This is a pivotal moment of awakening. Do you find yourself committed to something the Word of God forbids? Are you not doing something the Word of God requires? The Word confronts us with a choice that has the power to affect our destiny, our children's destiny, our bloodline for generations to come, the world, and the Kingdom. When we yield to Christ the potential for good is amazing. When we willfully disobey Christ, the consequences can be catastrophic. We live out our discipleship on the cutting edge of our choices.

If we remain submitted to 2 Timothy 3:16 then verse 17 will come to pass in our life!

[17]God uses it to prepare and equip his people to do every good work.

One more thought for this critical juncture. God loves you. His ways are always right, true, and good. Trust Him so you may have the faith and courage to obey Him. He has your best interest at heart. Your emotions, physical desires, opinions, and plans might seem right. If they go against the clear and consistent teaching of Gods' Word they are wrong. This is the moment on the journey when destinies are decided. Choose for God every time you reach this fork in your road. You will never be sorry.

A True Story About My Grand Daughter:

I was at church a few weeks ago when I saw my three-year-old granddaughter trying to stick her mother's car keys into an electric plug. It would have been funny except for the terrible potential for damage to her precious little hands. I have cut live electric wires and there is a melted spot in the blade of my favorite knife to prove it. My grandfather had one arm because his other was burned off attempting to pull his partner off a high-power line. When I saw the key going into the plug I knew immediately what could happen. My granddaughter did not. I bent down. Took away the keys. And told her "NO" in an appropriately stern voice. I explained this could hurt her so she should not do it. She jumped up and ran through the sanctuary crying and yelling about the fact that Poppie had told her "NO" and taken the keys away. How often do we do the same thing with God? I love my granddaughter and did what was best for her. She was just not buying it!

5.   The Word of God is dangerous. Christianity is a contact sport. The truth of God has the power to cause division. Throughout the centuries Christians have died or gone to prison for living and proclaiming their faith. It is still happening today in many parts of the world!   [Visit: www.persecution.com.]

A.   Acts 7:51-59 tells the story of the first N.T. martyr. Most believers will never find themselves in a situation this dramatic. However, it does show us how divisive the Word of God can be. Are you confident enough in Christ that you would choose to die rather than deny?

_____

_____

B.   Jesus warned His disciples how the world would respond to them, and why. Have you ever experienced this in your life? John 15:18-20

_____

_____

_____

6.   The good news is God's Word promises blessings as well as challenges.

Exodus 20:4-6 contains a portion of the Ten Commandments. Reflect upon the blessing in verse six. How might this apply to you and your family?

_____

_____

_____

_____

7.   John 6:66-69 contains one of the saddest and one of the most glorious verses in the Bible. Jesus had just finished a difficult teaching. In response to His teaching different people go different directions. What does Peter choose? Why?

_____

_____

8.   Psalm 19:9-11 captures the power of the promises in God's Word, or God's Law. What do they promise?

A.   _____

B.   _____

9.   Psalm 119 describes the attributes and promises of God's Word. Its 176 verses make it the longest chapter in the entire Bible. Its unique structure reveals itself in the original Hebrew because it follows the order of the entire Hebrew alphabet. Set aside time to read this Psalm, and put a check mark by the verses which speak to you in a special way. This Psalm makes many marvelous declarations. They speak

to many areas of life. Allow them to speak into your life and encourage you! Share the verses that speak to you with your mentor.

_____

_____

_____

Draw what Psalm 119 looks and feels like to you.

10. Ezra was a leader and a preacher in ancient Israel. He helped restore the law and worship to God's people at a key time in their history. Ezra 7:10 gives us a wonderful progression for leadership! What three things did Ezra do? In what order did he do them? Why was this order important?

1. _____

2. _____

3. _____

Do spiritual leaders today get into trouble if they violate this pattern? Why or why not?

_____

_____

_____

11. James 1:19-25 gives us a tremendously practical picture of our relationship to God's Word. What does James call us to do? What are the benefits if we obey?

_____

_____

_____

Does James follow the pattern of Ezra? How?

_____

_____

_____

12. We have said many times that these Sessions barely scratch the surface of subjects that deserve a lifetime of study. This is especially true of this Session. This topic is the key to all the others. Close your time by reflecting on these two verses. One is especially for believers. One is for seekers. Our prayer is that you will heed these words and make them a foundational principle of your life!

For the Believer: 2 Timothy 2:15 (KJV)
Study to show thyself approved unto God,
a workman that needeth not to be ashamed,
rightly dividing [correctly handling]
the word of truth.

For the Seeker: Acts 17:11-12 (NLT)
And the people of Berea were more open-minded
than those in Thessalonica,
and they listened eagerly to Paul's message.
They searched the Scriptures day after day
to see if Paul and Silas were teaching the truth.
As a result, many Jews believed,
as did many of the prominent Greek women and men.

Conclusion:

The Word of the Lord has the power to convict, save, transform, and equip. It has the power to heal, help, and encourage. It also has the power to confront, disquiet, and destroy. The Word of God can be a feather bed to catch the falling or a hammer to crush the arrogant rebel. God's Word has a message for any occasion or situation. However, it is like a gold mine. In order to find the nuggets, you must acquire the correct tools and be willing to sweat while you do some digging.

We live in a high-speed sound bite world. Most of us skim the Yahoo headlines, text, talk, and read the scrolling news alerts on the bottom of our TV, all at the same time. God's Word is just the opposite. It takes focused, intentional, time and effort. It takes spiritual hunger, diligent study, and tenacious persistence.

It welcomes the hungry spiritual baby who is willing to snuggle in, cuddle up, latch on, and drink deeply from its life-giving pages. The hungry ones will reap the rewards God promises in this life and eternal life in the age to come.

Military Training: "Interdicting their supply lines."

When I was in Special Forces training, we learned a key guerrilla warfare principle. The way a smaller and weaker fighting force defeats a large conventional force is by "Interdicting their supply lines." That means you burn their food, blow up their bridges, mine their landing strips, burn up their fuel supply, and explode their ammunition depot. If your enemy is cold, hungry, thirsty, immobile, and unarmed they cannot fight effectively. Satan is a brilliant strategist. He will do everything possible to, "Interdict your spiritual supply line." If he can keep you out of the Word, he has separated you from your sword! You will eventually become too weak to fight effectively. If you find yourself facing a never-ending string of excuses for missing worship, small group, mentoring, or Bible study you can be certain God is not sending them. Satan has cut your supply line. Do whatever you must to get it back. Do it now.

Jumpstart Mentoring 5

"The Sword"

Checking In:

If you are a mature believer this week probably encouraged things you already believe. If you are a new believer you may have been shocked by the authority the Word of God claims. When I was a baby Christian, John Gosset did Bible study with me at the Helen Street Church of Christ in Fayetteville, N.C. We would sit in his kitchen and open our Dixon KJV Study Bibles. He would pick a topic like God, Jesus, sin, or sanctification. We used the verses in the concordance at the back of the Bible to guide our studies. Those were precious times that introduced me to the study of God's Word. John was very clear with me. I now belonged to Jesus. He was my Lord. His Word was now my guide. This was a shocking new experience for me! Forty years later I look back with a grateful heart and know he was right. Share honestly with your mentor about your reaction to this week's Session. Accepting the absolute authority of God's written Word will be one of the most important discipleship decisions you every make! Without it you run the risk of recreating Jesus in your image.

Conversation Starters:

1. Go back to the Preface Question on the milk of the Word. Which of the five types best describes you? Why?

_____

_____

_____

2. The idea of change runs through the Scriptures. God calls Christians to be conformed to the "image" of Christ. How does this idea strike you? Do you see yourself as a piece of clay in the hands of God? Are you willing to be "made over?"

_____

_____

3. Key in and spend time with question 3. Share your answers with one another. This question puts teeth in the fundamental issue. Are you Lord of your life and setting the agenda? Or, is God Lord of your life?

_____

_____

4.   Questions 4 and 5 look at the power and the peril of God's Word. Has obeying
        God's Word ever gotten you into hot water? Are there any areas of your life where
        you are holding the Word, "at arm's length?"

        _____

5.   Question 9 invited you to read Psalm 119 with pen in hand. What verses did you
        mark? What was it in these verses that spoke to your heart? Share them together.

        _____

        _____

        _____

        _____

6.   What leadership pattern did Ezra and James teach us in questions 10 and 11?
        How are you putting this into practice in your own life?
        If you are a parent, how can you help your children engage this pattern?

        _____

        _____

        _____

OIKOS:

When Paul was a baby Christian he went to a gathering and had a conversation with one of the men. When he got home his mother called and asked him, "What did you do to him?" Paul had not done anything to him. He had simply engaged him in conversation and shared some things God was doing in his own life. Sadly, the man was completely freaked out by the encounter. Time reveled the man was a drunk who was having an affair and heading for divorce. Paul did not know anything at the time. Yet, the Word of God and the Spirit of God worked together and brought conviction to the man's soul. Be prepared for the possibility God in you will begin to reveal Himself to your OIKOS through you. Some may like it while others may not. Be kind, gentle, and loving. The work is God's, not yours. All you need do is abide in His Word. Your light will shine and people will see it. What they do with it is between them and God.

Closing Reflection:

When you put a fresh white carnation into a vase with red food coloring something happens. The color flows up the stem and into the petals. The flower absorbs the color and changes forever. The same is true of God's Word in you. So soak it up.

Jesus taught us in John 8:31-32 (NLT),
"You are truly my disciples if you remain faithful to my teachings.
And you will know the truth,
and the truth will set you free."

The Lord spoke to Jeremiah the prophet in Jeremiah 18:1-6 (NLT),

The LORD gave another message to Jeremiah. He said,
"Go down to the potter's shop, and I will speak to you there."
So I did as he told me and found the potter working at his wheel.
But the jar he was making did not turn out as he had hoped,
so he crushed it into a lump of clay again and started over.
Then the LORD gave me this message:
"O Israel, can I not do to you as this potter has done to his clay?
As the clay is in the potter's hand, so are you in my hand.

Press in hard to the truth of God. Give all you are to all you know God to be. Do not quit! Do not back off! When God shows you something own it, accept it, and do it! Sparks can fly when God begins to put new things into your life or take old things out. Allow the Word of God, and the Spirit of God, to pierce you all the way through. Lay on your back in the hand of God while He cleans you. Stay in the oven of God until your biscuits are golden brown, even if you feel the flames!

Prayer Guide:

Heavenly Father:
Fill our hearts and minds with a hunger for Your Word.
Keep the evil one far from us, protect our supply lines,
and grant us great diligence to study Your Word.
Open our minds that we might understand
and soften our hearts so we may receive and obey.
Steel our will and grant us great fortitude
to persist in all You call us to.
Conform us to the image of Jesus Christ in all things.
Let us be the baby, the flower, the clay, the fish, and the biscuit.
Continue Your work in us until we are complete.
In Jesus mighty name we pray, Amen

Jumpstart Session 6

"The Connection"

Introduction:

I do not know the president of any country who would allow me to walk into their office and start sharing my inner most thoughts. The King of the Universe does just that! He invites us to enter His throne room and talk to Him. In fact, He delights in our fellowship. This week we are going to examine some of the different dimensions of prayer God made available to us through Christ. You will also see the amazing role the Holy Spirit plays on your behalf! Open your heart and mind to this amazing opportunity!

Key Verses for Memorization and Reflection: Psalm 116:2 (NLT)
Because he bends down to listen,
I will pray as long as I have breath!

Lesson:

There are 468 verses about prayer in the NLT. They begin in Genesis and run all the way through the Revelation. You find prayer in the law, prophets, kings, Psalms, gospels, and epistles. Every great spiritual leader has spoken with God. More importantly, God has spoken to them. Thankfully, prayer is not just for the great and mighty. God welcomes each one of us. No matter how strong, weak, or wise we may be.

1. Begin your study with Luke 6:12. Whom do we find spending a night in prayer to God? What thoughts or questions come to mind when you think of this person spending time in prayer with God?

_____

_____

2. The disciples saw a consistent pattern of prayer in the life of Jesus. He prayed by Himself. He prayed with the disciples. He pulled Peter, James, and John aside for special prayer times. He prayed for lunch in the presence of thousands. He even prayed for the sick and the dead. As the disciples saw the regular pattern of prayer in the life of Jesus they came to see their own need. They asked him "Lord, teach us to pray." Jesus responded with His famous teaching found in Matthew 6:5-13 (NLT)! Use those verses to answer the following questions.

A.   What does Jesus think about "showing off" prayers?
"When you pray, don't be like the hypocrites who love to pray publicly
on street corners and in the synagogues where everyone can see them.
I tell you the truth, that is all the reward they will ever get.

_____

_____

B.   What attitude should we have when we pray?

But when you pray,
go away by yourself, shut the door behind you,
and pray to your Father in private. Then your Father,
who sees everything, will reward you.

_____

_____

C.   What does Jesus think of repeated words and an empty heart?
"When you pray, don't babble on and on as people of other religions do.
They think their prayers are answered merely by repeating their words
again and again. Don't be like them, for your Father knows
exactly what you need even before you ask him!

_____

_____

D.   One of the biggest challenges to your relationship with God may be your
relationship with your earthly father. How does the idea of talking to your
Heavenly Father connect with your memories of speaking to your earthly father?
Is there any heart healing needing to happen as you learn to share with Father God?

Example:

If your earthly father yelled and screamed it might take time to realize your Heavenly
Father loves and listens. If your earthly father lied or stole from you it might take time to
realize God is truthful and trustworthy. If your earthly father ever abused or misused,
your Heavenly Father would love to heal your heart and show you what true love looks
and feels like. I am praying for you as you walk with Jesus through this painful process.

Pray like this: Our Father in heaven

E.   What does it mean to you that Jesus called God your "Father in heaven?"
For some this is a positive thing, for others it might be a painful stumbling block.

_____

_____

_____

"may your name be kept holy."

F.   When we enter into God's presence we are on Holy Ground.
Are you ready for His Holiness to rub off on you? Are your friends ready?

_____

_____

May your Kingdom come soon.
May your will be done on earth, as it is in heaven.

G.   What will it mean for you and your OIKOS if the values of God and His Kingdom begin to take shape in your day-to-day life? What will it look like when you truly seek to "do His will" all the time?

_____

_____

_____

[11]Give us today the food we need,

H.   God cares about your needs! What specific and tangible needs can you lift up to your caring and loving Father? This truth goes well beyond food! What life needs do you have that only God can touch?

_____

_____

_____

and forgive us our sins, as we have forgiven those who sin against us.

I.	There is a clear and direct relational aspect to prayer! Jesus connected God forgiving our sins with us forgiving those who have sinned against us. We talked in Session one about how Adam's sin caused him to hide from God. We established that sin separates us from God, others, and our own true self. God invites you to forgive others and to receive His forgiveness. What roadblocks might you have in either earthly or heavenly relationships? What steps is God calling you to take?

_____

_____

_____

And don't let us yield to temptation, but rescue us from the evil one.

J.	There is a devil whom Christ called the tempter. The evil one is outside of us. Temptation works within and without. Are there forces outside of yourself from which you need protection? What inner temptations does God need to touch in your life?

_____

_____

Remember:

It is easier to pray for strength when you are working out at the gym than when you are standing in line at the buffet. Part of praying for deliverance from temptation is getting honest and admitting who tempts us, what tempts us, and where we go to get tempted. I am a professional rat trapper. My grandfather taught me how to set a rat trap with extra crunchy peanut butter. It is not really fair. If a hungry rat enters my garage he is mine. Satan is no different. He knows what you crave and once you get lost in the bait it is too late. He has you. The key to being free is staying out of the garage.

3.	What conditions does Peter give us for answered prayer?

A.	1 Peter 1:17	_____

B.	1 Peter 3:7	_____

C.	1 Peter 3:10-12	_____

4.	Daniel was an amazing O.T. prophet. God used him to influence the rulers of heavenly and earthly kingdoms. Look at his story, and learn principles you can put into practice.

A.   How seriously did Daniel take prayer? Daniel 6:6-11

_____

_____

B.   Can you hear the passion for his people in Daniels prayer?
      What cause stirs your heart to petition God in prayer like this? Daniel 9:17-19

_____

_____

_____

C.   When Daniel prayed on earth what happened in heaven? Daniel 9:20-23

_____

_____

D.   Daniel 10:12-14 paints an amazing picture of war in the heavenly realm. Can you
      imagine a satanic being blocking a heavenly messenger? Meditate on this passage!
      Do you see yourself as a cosmic warrior? Do you believe your prayers release war
      in the heavens over your house, family, church, city, and country? They do!

Then he said, "Don't be afraid, Daniel.
Since the first day you began to pray for understanding
and to humble yourself before your God,
your request has been heard in heaven.
I have come in answer to your prayer.
But for twenty-one days the spirit prince of the kingdom of Persia
blocked my way.
Then Michael, one of the archangels, came to help me,
and I left him there with the spirit prince of the kingdom of Persia.
Now I am here to explain what will happen to your people in the future,
for this vision concerns a time yet to come."

_____

_____

_____

_____

5.   I want you to think about the most challenging issues you face. Think about your marriage, job, kids, finances, health, and ministry. Think about your greatest hopes, fears, and dreams. Let your mind wander. Ask the Holy Spirit to pray for you and protect you as you seek His guidance for your prayer needs. When your need is clear move to the words of Jesus in Luke to receive a great promise.
Read Luke 11:5-13. What is Jesus saying to you about your need right now?

_____

_____

6.   What does Jesus say about persistence in prayer in Luke 18:1-6?

_____

_____

7.   Here are a few verses which have encouraged me on my prayer journey!
Read them slowly. Think them through. Apply them to your life right now.
How do they encourage you in light of challenges you may be facing?

A.   Jeremiah 33:3

_____

_____

B.   Romans 8:26-27

_____

_____

_____

_____

C.   Revelation 5:8

_____

_____

D.   Revelation 8:3-4

_____

_____

8.   The writer of the book of Hebrews gives us a great declaration about our Lord and Savior, Jesus the Christ! It is an amazing invitation that many people of faiths other than Christianity can scarcely understand. Sadly, some churches have built layers of leadership between God, and His people. Claim the following verses for your very own and never allow anyone, or anything, to take them away from you.

Hebrews 10:19-23 (NLT)
"And so, dear brothers and sisters,
we can boldly enter heaven's Most Holy Place
because of the blood of Jesus.
By his death, Jesus opened a new and life-giving way
through the curtain into the Most Holy Place.
And since we have a great High Priest who rules over God's house,
let us go right into the presence of God
with sincere hearts fully trusting him.
For our guilty consciences have been sprinkled with Christ's blood
to make us clean, and our bodies have been washed with pure water.
Let us hold tightly without wavering to the hope we affirm,
for God can be trusted to keep his promise."

A.   Who or what gives you the authority to enter the very throne room of God?

_____

_____

B.   What should your attitude be as you approach the King?

_____

_____

C.   If Jesus paid the price and made the way do you need any other religious leader or institution to open the door and make a way?

_____

_____

_____

D. Is there any mention of paying money to gain access to God?

_____

_____

_____

Conclusion:

A classic old hymn gives us an awesome invitation:

**To God be the glory, great things He hath done,
So loved He the world that He gave us His Son,
Who yielded His life an atonement for sin,
And opened the life-gate that all may go in.
All come to the Father, through Jesus the Son,
And give Him the glory; great things He hath done.
Fanny Jane Crosby (1820-1915)**

Prayer is a conversation. It is the small child climbing boldly into their mother's lap and the teenager having a sincere heart to heart with dad. It is the ambassador reporting to their president for instructions. It is an attorney begging the judge to show mercy.

Prayer is wonderfully simple and available to the youngest child. Prayer is powerful communication capable of unleashing war in the heavens. Prayer is open to all because of the work Jesus Christ finished upon the cross. Prayer also puts demands on our character and calls for obedience to God. Prayer is the vital link to our living Lord! Explore it for yourself with humility, passion, and persistence! Only God knows where the journey of prayer will take you!

If you ever become stuck in your prayer life, ask the Holy Spirit to help you. Remember, we do not even know how to pray as we should. The Spirit can read our mind, know our heart, and groan our innermost thoughts before the throne of God. He does it in such an amazing way we are known and heard completely and absolutely. So, take heart and reach out! God is always ready to connect.

Jumpstart Mentoring 6

"The Connection"

Conversation Starters:

1. Were you raised in a praying family? Is it part of your tradition and experience?

   _____

   _____

2. If not your family, who introduced you to prayer? When and where?

   _____

   _____

3. Can you think of a time when God specifically answered prayer in a definitive way?

   _____

   _____

4. Look back through the Session. Go over your answers together. Is there a special teaching, character, or concept that really grabbed you?

   _____

   _____

5.   Is prayer a regular part of your life? If not, what can you do to begin the habit of praying?

_____

_____

6.   We spoke about the connection between parents, especially fathers, and our view of God. Did this connect with you in a way you are willing to share? Be very gentle, kind, and tender in this area. Hurtful memories of the past can be painful, especially if they have never been shared before. I pray God makes you brave, and heals anything it is time to share. Read the reflection below as part of this question.

_____

_____

The Reality of Abuse:

Some years ago, I was doing a story writing exercise with a group of leaders. I will not even hint at what, where, or who for the sake of total privacy. If you were there you know who you are. Please maintain everyone's privacy if you recognize this story. I love each of you very much! And I am so proud of who you are.

We worked through an exercise in personal story writing. As you complete your trip down memory lane you write a personal narrative of the positive and negative things you have experienced in life. While we were working on our stories one woman jumped up and ran from the room. Little did I know what was to come. Later, as we read our stories I was astonished by the tales of rape, abuse, and molestation. Not just from the women, but from the men. Grown men of God wept as they told of being raped by a neighbor man as a child. Women wept as they shared stories they had never told anyone, ever. I sat and wept as I realized the depth of harm and pain these precious leaders had experienced. Let me say that again. These were Godly men and women who had been in God's work for many years. Yet for many, they had never let their most terrible secrets out. It was God's time to begin their healing process.

I realize I am treading on Holy and horrible ground right now. But if God brought you here for this moment of healing, then I pray you trust your mentor and walk through the door. Abuser or abused, it does not matter. Share your pain and let God heal your heart. Open a new door with your Heavenly Father and taste what healing and freedom can be. It is a journey. But it begins with a step of trust. I love you, and I am praying for you right now! If this reflection connects with any of you precious daughters of God, please go to www.hopeafterbetrayal.com and tell Meg JumpStart sent you. She will understand.

7.   Take some time to pray together right now. Consider making a list of the things that are currently on your heart and mind. Write them down. Talk to God about them. Continue to lift them up to God in prayer, and then keep a record of what happens in regard to each one of them. Keeping a written prayer list with a record of the answers can be a tremendous faith builder. Just be wise and careful how you write and store sensitive requests. I often write prayers in code that only I can understand.

_____

_____

_____

_____

OIKOS:

You have spent the week studying several aspects of prayer. Some of your best opportunities for prayer are already surrounding you. God has sovereignly and wonderfully placed people in your OIKOS. In future Sessions we will talk about loving them, serving them, and sharing the gospel with them. Today you can begin by praying for them. Write the names of those God has placed around you. Pick your closest eight to fifteen people. Then begin to pray for them. Ask God to draw them and reveal Himself to them. You will be amazed to see what can happen when you bathe your OIKOS in prayer.

Closing Reflection:

Again, you have touched the tip of the iceberg. Keep saying your prayers. Use the model of Jesus. Have the persistence of Daniel. Claim the promises. If you would like something encouraging and challenging for your soul listen to this sermon by Pastor Jim Cymbala of the Brooklyn Tabernacle. The link is still active as of 10/2016.

www.youtube.com/watch?v=U79YOKje2zU

Prayer Guide:

Heavenly Father:
I come to you in the name of Jesus and ask You to send the Holy
Spirit to teach me how to pray. I would like to know You,
experience You, and hear Your voice.
I desire to open all of who I am to all of who you are.
Please allow the prayer You gave Saint Paul
to find fulfillment in my life, Amen

When I think of all this, I fall to my knees and pray to the Father,
the Creator of everything in heaven and on earth.
I pray that from his glorious, unlimited resources he will
empower you with inner strength through his Spirit.
Then Christ will make his home in your hearts as you trust in him.
Your roots will grow down into God's love and keep you strong.
And may you have the power to understand,
as all God's people should,
how wide, how long, how high, and how deep his love is.
May you experience the love of Christ,
though it is too great to understand fully.
Then you will be made complete with all the fullness of life
and power that comes from God.
Now all glory to God, who is able,
through his mighty power at work within us,
to accomplish infinitely more than we might ask or think.
Glory to him in the church and in Christ Jesus
through all generations forever and ever! Amen.
Ephesians 3:14-21 (NLT)

Jumpstart Session 7

"The Invitation"

Introduction:

I heard a joke about football and church being very much alike. Because, on Sunday people who need exercise sit in the seats and watch tired people who need a rest! The awesome truth is God has work for each of His children to do. Church is not about the rested saints watching the exhausted leaders run around. The true church is all about leaders, called and equipped by God, raising up, training, and releasing an army of disciples! All of God's people are invited! How awesome! You have an important part to play in the Body of Christ.

Key Verses for Memorization and Reflection: Ephesians 2:10 (NLT)
For we are God's masterpiece. [KJV: His Workmanship]
He has created us anew in Christ Jesus,
so we can do the good things he planned for us long ago.

___

Lesson:

All too often, the church appears to be a place where people go to watch the show! The place where sinful people sit in the seats and watch the holy professional lay the smack down! Nothing is farther from the truth. God has uniquely gifted and called every one of His precious children into service. Next week we will look at the wonderful diversity of spiritual gifts at work within the Body of Christ. Today we are going to focus on every believer's call! Allow God's Word, not church tradition, to define your place in the Body.

1.   Check out Mark 1:16-20.

A.   What call did Jesus give to the disciples?

_____

_____

B.   What did Jesus promise to teach them, or make them, if they followed?

_____

_____

C.   What did the disciples do?

_____

D.   How do you think the people who were left behind felt about what had just
      happened? Might the future disciples have felt torn? How would you have felt?

_____

_____

2.   1 Peter 4:10 is a great declaration! It tells us what God has given us, and what we
      are to do with it! Pay special attention to the words, "each of you."

A.   What does God give every believer?

_____

B.   What are you to do with God's gifts?

_____

_____

3.   The Apostle Paul gives us a great pattern for harmony and ministry in the Body of
      Christ.

Romans 12:6-8 (NLT)
In his grace, God has given us different gifts for doing certain things well.
So if God has given you the ability to prophesy,
speak out with as much faith as God has given you.
If your gift is serving others, serve them well.
If you are a teacher, teach well.
If your gift is to encourage others, be encouraging.
If it is giving, give generously.
If God has given you leadership ability,
take the responsibility seriously.
And if you have a gift for showing kindness to others, do it gladly.

A.   Does everyone have the same call and gifting?

_____

_____

_____

B.   Paul mentions several different gifts. After each gift, he describes an action or an attitude that describes how we should use the gift. Which words are they?

_____

_____

C.   Which of these words best describes your commitment to serve God?

_____

_____

4.   Matthew 25:14-28 is a very famous parable about our faithfulness with the gifts, talents, and abilities God gives us. Read the story and pay special attention to what the master tells each servant. As you read the story, think about your participation in the Kingdom of God.

A.   Are you one of the "well done" servants? Why?

_____

_____

_____

B.   Are you in the "I was afraid and buried my talent" group? Why?

_____

_____

5.   Now, we are going to examine a foundational portion of God's Word. This Scripture defines my understanding of the pastor's main role in a church. Enjoy!

Give Ephesians 4:11-12 & 16 (NLT) an extra careful reading because it is so important. It may challenge your view of your pastor's real role in the church.

A.   What gifts did God give to the church?

Now these are the gifts Christ gave to the church:
the apostles, the prophets, the evangelists, and the pastors and teachers.

_____

_____

_____

B.	If you are one of these unique gifts that Christ gave to His church what is your job? If you are one of God's people what is your job?

> **Their responsibility is to equip God's people
> to do his work and build up the church, the body of Christ.**

_____

_____

_____

C.	Reflect on verse 16. You are unique, special, and important to the cause of Christ and the Body of Christ! What happens in the church "if each part does its own special work"?

> **He makes the whole body fit together perfectly.
> As each part does its own special work, it helps the other parts grow,
> so that the whole body is healthy and growing and full of love.**

_____

_____

_____

D.	Let's ask verse 16 in reverse. What do you think happens in the church if God's people do not take their place, play their part, and use their gifts?

_____

_____

_____

Reflection:

Many churches follow a traditional manmade pattern for ministry. A man or a woman goes off to school and "Learns to be a minister." When that person graduates they return to the local church where they spend their life "Doing the ministry." The paid professional is so good at doing the ministry they can gather a faithful flock of tithing followers. Over time a splendid co-dependent relationship develops. The pastor loves being the minister, and the people love receiving ministry. This ruins God's glorious plan for His church.

God gave apostles, prophets, evangelists, and pastor/teachers as gifts to His church so they would use their gifts to equip all the saints of God to use their gifts. The local church pastor is not a minister. Christ gave them to the church to equip the saints for the work of their ministry. God gives gifts to all of His children. God has work for all of His children to do. When all of God's children are using the gifts God gave them for the common good amazing things will happen. Church members must set their pastors free from the traditional duties of ministers, so they can do the real pastoral work of "Equipping the saints for the work of their ministries." Ask your pastor to be a trainer, not just the doer.

6.   What authority does every Christian have to serve God and use their gifts? We have looked at the clear call to participation in the verses above. Now St. Peter is going to tell you just who you are in Christ! Remember the Word of God always trumps tradition. Allow Peter to define your position in Christ.

1 Peter 2:4,5,9B (NLT)
You are coming to Christ, who is the living cornerstone of God's temple.
He was rejected by people, but he was chosen by God for great honor.
And you are living stones that God is building into his spiritual temple.

What's more, you are his holy priests.
Through the mediation of Jesus Christ,
you offer spiritual sacrifices that please God.

For you are a chosen people.
You are royal priests, a holy nation, God's very own posession.
9B As a result, you can show others the goodness of God,
for he called you out of the darkness into his wonderful light.

Peter is writing to all believers in this passage. Look carefully at the words he uses.

You are living stones, holy priests, chosen people,
royal priests, and God's very own.

God has called you, anointed you, appointed you, gifted you, and placed you.
Nobody has the right to deprive you of the glorious call, position,
or ministry God has for you!

According to Peter, what qualifies you to show others the goodness of God? [Verse 9B]

_____

_____

_____

7.   Before we close this Session we are going to look at a beautiful O.T. example of God calling a leader to share the anointing and the ministry with the people he is leading. We will trace the story from Numbers 11 in the O.T. all the way to Acts 2 in the N.T.

A.   Read Numbers 11:10-15. Was Moses having fun leading the children of Israel? Why do you think so?

_____

_____

B.   What was God's solution? [Verses 16-17]

_____

_____

_____

C.   What did God do? [Verses 24-25]

_____

_____

D.   Now read verses 26-30.

       Why was Joshua worried?

_____

_____

       What was Moses response and attitude?

_____

_____

Thought:

Moses was not worried about his ego or position. He wanted the people of God to receive all God had for them. He was secure enough in himself not to care who God used. Moses cried out with the heart of a true leader. He wanted God's spirit for all of God's people. He wanted God to use all of them to His glory. Moses prayer came true on the day of Pentecost when the Holy Spirit anointed the believers and fulfilled the prophecy of Joel.

No, what you see was predicted long ago by the prophet Joel:
'In the last days,' God says, 'I will pour out my Spirit upon all people.
Your sons and daughters will prophesy.

Your young men will see visions, and your old men will dream dreams.
In those days I will pour out my Spirit even on my servants—
men and women alike— and they will prophesy.
Acts 2:16-18 (NLT)

Conclusion:

It is important for believers to grow in ministry faith and skill. Christians should be lifelong learners. However, the Lord did not call us to serve because of our skill and knowledge. Christ called us out of darkness into the light by His grace. The Holy Spirit gave us gifts to use in service to the world, and the church. God gave us the role of priests in the house of Christ. Everything we have comes by the grace of God. The great truth is God has called, gifted, and placed each of His children in the Body of Christ according to His good purpose. When each of us does our work under the blessing and anointing of Christ the church grows and prospers. It is an awesome plan.

God is looking for two clear responses from each of you.
First, is your willingness to say with the prophet Isaiah, "Here am I Lord, send me!"
Second, is your faithfulness to use what God has given you for His glory.

Luke 19:17 (NLT)
"'Well done!' the king exclaimed. 'You are a good servant.
You have been faithful with the little I entrusted to you,
so you will be governor of ten cities as your reward.'"

1 Corinthians 4:2 (NLT)
Now, a person who is put in charge
as a manager must be faithful.

Christ has saved us, called us, and gifted us. He has work for us to do! He is asking us to trust Him, follow Him, obey Him, and be faithful. He knew what He was doing when He placed you in His Body the Church! Do not be afraid to put your gifts into service. Only God knows what will happen if you step out in faith and do what He is calling you to do! I believe your Mentor, Life Group Leader, and Pastor will be thrilled when you step up and say, "I am ready to serve. Teach me and help me find my place."

REMEMBER:

We try, we fail, we learn,
and hopefully do better next time!

My dad taught me to ski
when I was five years old.
He told me repeatedly,
"If you are not falling, you are not trying!"

The important thing is to keep trying.
Get back up when you fall down.
Keep learning, keep serving!
Someday you will get it right,
or at least get better.

The glory does not belong to you anyway!

God will take your best efforts,
touch them with His power and glory,
and use them to accomplish amazing things!

You are a valuable and precious member
of the living Body of Jesus Christ.

Never allow any person to keep you from doing
what God has called and gifted you to do!

Jumpstart Mentoring 7

"The Invitation"

Checking In:

In the next Session, you will look at the spiritual gifts God gives to help you do the work He has called you to do. Today is the perfect time to start talking with your mentor about serving in your local church. Share your past experiences of serving in the church. If you are new to church life take time and share what God's call means to you. I know the "Priesthood of all believers" can challenge some religious traditions. So, always allow God's Word to be the final Word. Beware anyone who tries to stand between you and God, or to limit your use of the gifts God has given you. So long as you are using them decently and in order. Under the rightful guidance of your churches leaders. If they won't allow you to serve, ask them why!

Conversation Starters:

1. Think about past church experiences you have had. Have you been an involved participant or a passive spectator?

_____

_____

2. Go back and look over the Session. What verses, or questions, caught your attention? What did they say to you? How did they challenge you?

_____

3. Go back to question #5. What is the unique role of the pastor, and what is the amazing role of every member of the Body of Christ? What freedom does this give you? What responsibility comes with it?

_____

4. Now go back to question #6. What authority does God's Word give you?

_____

_____

5. Is there any job, or ministry, you have desired to do in your church, chapel, or faith community? Talk to your mentor about ways you can become involved.

_____

_____

_____

_____

Thought:

I want to celebrate how God calls and gifts each of His children. Work with the leaders of your local church. They should gladly help you grow and explore areas of ministry. It is especially important to realize you are unique and special. Every person who pays the bills, cooks the food, cleans the bathrooms, folds the bulletin, teaches the children, or preaches the message on Sunday morning is critical for the effective work of the local church. When all God's people use their gifts, talents, and abilities the church is powerful indeed. I am praying God opens new and amazing areas of service for you. There is nothing more exciting than serving Christ and His people.

OIKOS:

As you begin to see yourself as a servant of God I pray He opens your eyes to the mission field around you. One of the most powerful tools for impacting the world is service. I may not agree with your theology, but I will probably accept a cup of cold water on a hot day. We are living in a world where people can be afraid of one another. You know God has already given you a special circle of influence to serve. Last week you began praying for your OIKOS. This week I challenge you to begin looking for ways to serve your OIKOS. I pray your OIKOS has noticed the change in your spirit. I pray they attend your baptism. I pray they are sensing God working in their lives as a result of your influence. And now I pray God allows you to love on your OIKOS through service and good deeds.

Closing Reflection:

Nike says, "Just Do It."
Uncle Sam says, "I Want You!"

Jesus says, "If you will follow Me I will make you a fisher of men." He has called you, saved you, gifted you, and placed you in His Body the Church. He desires you to trust Him, and use the gifts He has given you. More than anything else, Jesus is asking you to be faithful! If you will be faithful and willing, God will use you to His glory! Do the best you can do, with what you have, where you are, and leave the rest to God!

Jumpstart Session 8

"The Equipping"

Introduction:

Spiritual gifts are one of the most important and misunderstood areas in modern church life. It is not surprising the enemy takes something potentially powerful for the advance of the Kingdom and turns it into an issue which causes civil war in His church. This week we are going to look at the wonderful list of gifts the Lord uses to equip His people. I promise you from the beginning we will not force anything upon you or try to take anything away from you! Enjoy this journey of discovery. I pray you see something in a new way!

Key Verses for Memorization and Reflection: 1 Corinthians 12:7 (NLT)
A spiritual gift is given to each of us so we can help each other.

Lesson:

This week we will look at the primary N.T. lists of spiritual gifts. We will answer the key question, "Who is the giver and assigner of the gifts?" We will divide the gifts and look at them according to our personality. My prayer is this lesson encourages your exploration of spiritual gifts and takes away some of the tension which can divide the Body of Christ over this awesome topic. Enjoy the journey.

Thirty years ago, at Azusa Pacific University,
my mentor Dr. Bruce Baloian
shared a saying I have never forgotten.
"You cannot put the Holy Spirit in a box
and you cannot make Him dance!"
Some Christians get into trouble when
they build a theology based on
what they think the Spirit must do.
Others err by deciding what the Spirit cannot do!
Both extremes lead us astray.
Do not put Him in a box
or try to make Him dance!

1.   Let's begin by having you create your own list of spiritual gifts. Use the lists in Romans 12:6-8 and 1 Corinthians 12:8-10 & 27-28. You may find duplicates, so only list each gift once.

_____   _____
_____   _____
_____   _____
_____   _____
_____   _____
_____   _____
_____   _____
_____   _____
_____   _____
_____   _____
_____   _____
_____   _____
_____   _____

2.   1 Peter 4:11A gives us two categories for spiritual gift. Peter talks about speaking and helping. Another translation talks about words and serving. Here is the very important point. Some of us like to get up front and talk. Others like to bake the cookies for the potluck. All our gifts are important to the Body of Christ. We need good preaching, Life Notes, hot coffee, and somebody to balance the checkbook. All the gifts are important and all God's children are gifted. Nobody is better than anybody else in the Body of Christ! You are each special and essential.

1 Peter 4:11 (NLT)
Do you have the gift of speaking?
Then speak as though God himself were speaking through you.
Do you have the gift of helping others?
Do it with all the strength and energy that God supplies.
Then everything you do will bring glory to God through Jesus Christ.
All glory and power to him forever and ever! Amen.

Go back to the list you created in question one. Put a **T** beside the gifts that involve talking. Put an **S** beside the gifts primarily for serving. After you have sorted out the gifts do a little personal reflection. Are you primarily a talker or a server? Would you rather be speaking or doing something?

TALKING ☐   SERVING ☐

Here is another way to think about this. Imagine there are forty people sitting in the next room. They are ready and waiting. Would you rather stand in the back of the room and organize the book table, or would you rather go up front and tell them a story? Remember, both answers are right. Many of you will find one of these options exciting and the other boring or horrifying. Some will find both equally excellent. It's all good. I'm just trying to get you thinking about your personality type, who you are, what you like.

The great news is every ministry in the Body of Christ is important. I love to talk. Talking is easy for me, always has been. Just ask my grade school teachers who gave me Unsatisfactory in the Avoids Needless Talking category of my Report Card. I always disagreed, because I knew there was no such thing as Needless Talking. LOL. I praise God for the people in churches who play instruments, teach children, pay bills, set up the rooms, and usher. If nobody ran sound, lights, and video equipment on Sunday the worship service would be in deep trouble. Praise God for every folded bulletin and prepared meal. Praise God for every single gifted member. Always lift everybody up and don't ever put anybody down. We need every single one of you in the Body of Christ!

3. Who gets a gift? (Remember: If a question doesn't make sense try answering it from the NLT.)

A. 1 Peter 4:10

_____

_____

B.   Matthew 25:14   (View the talents, or money, as gifts.)

_____

_____

4.   Who is the giver of the gifts?

A.   1 Corinthians 12:4-6

_____

_____

B.   1 Corinthians 4:7

_____

_____

C.   Romans 12:6

_____

_____

5.   What should you do with the gifts and grace God has given you?

A.   Matthew 20:28

_____

_____

B.   1 Corinthians 15:10   [What is God's part, and what is yours?]

_____

_____

C.   Consider 1 Samuel 17:45-46. Does young David reveal the same two dynamics at work?

_____

_____

_____

6.   God did not give us gifts because of how cool and talented we are! There is a key word, which describes God's attitude toward your gifting in Romans 12:6A. What is it?

_____

_____

_____

Reflection:

When you repent of your sins and accept Jesus Christ as Lord and Savior He baptizes you into His Body the Church. The exciting thing about belonging to Jesus is He has work for you to do. God gives each of His children at least one powerful and specific spiritual gift. God gives us gifts because of His grace. He gives us gifts with the expectation that we will use them. Not for our ego or accolades. Not for wealth or position. God gives us His grace gifts so we will use them for the common good, for the building up of the Body of Christ. God has gifted you so you will serve others. It is just that simple, and powerful.

The amazing thing is you are unique, you are precious, and you are important. Together we are the Body of Christ. Just as your human body has many parts with different purposes so is the Body of Christ. Listen to the words of St. Paul as he describes this amazing unity within the Body of Christ. You are part of the Body he is speaking about.

1 Corinthians 12:12-26 (NLT)
The human body has many parts, but the many parts make up one whole body.
So it is with the body of Christ. Some of us are Jews,
some are Gentiles, some are slaves, and some are free.
But we have all been baptized into one body by one Spirit,
and we all share the same Spirit.

Yes, the body has many different parts, not just one part.
If the foot says, "I am not a part of the body because I am not a hand,
"that does not make it any less a part of the body.
And if the ear says,
"I am not part of the body because I am not an eye,
"would that make it any less a part of the body?
If the whole body were an eye, how would you hear?
Or if your whole body were an ear, how would you smell anything?
But our bodies have many parts,
and God has put each part just where he wants it.

How strange a body would be if it had only one part!
Yes, there are many parts, but only one body.
The eye can never say to the hand, "I don't need you.
"The head can't say to the feet,
"I don't need you."

In fact, some parts of the body that seem weakest
and least important are actually the most necessary.
And the parts we regard as less honorable are those we clothe
with the greatest care.
So we carefully protect those parts that should not be seen,
while the more honorable parts do not require this special care.
So God has put the body together such that extra honor and care
are given to those parts that have less dignity.
This makes for harmony among the members,
so that all the members care for each other.
If one part suffers, all the parts suffer with it,
and if one part is honored, all the parts are glad.

7.   What do the words of St. Paul above say to you about your place in the Body?
     Is there room for diversity in the Body?
     Is there room in the Body of Christ for you and your gifts?

_____

_____

_____

_____

8.   1 Corinthians 14:26 (NLT) gives us a wonderful benediction.

Well, my brothers and sisters, let's summarize.
When you meet together, one will sing, another will teach,
another will tell some special revelation God has given,
one will speak in tongues, and another will interpret what is said.
But everything that is done must strengthen all of you.

What is the key to the healthy use of spiritual gifts?

_____

_____

_____

_____

_____

Conclusion:

God gave each of you gifts to unify, not divide. Gifts used in mutual submission, love, and respect are a source of tremendous blessing for the Body of Christ. Gifts should not be scary or confusing. When the world sees gifts used properly they open eyes and hearts to the Lord who gave them.

If God gives gifts to your spiritual community He desires to see them used fully, decently, and in order. No person can pretend to give you any of the gifts. Because they cannot. Nor should any human deny the gifts. Because it is God who gives them.

OK ARTISTS, WHAT DO SPIRITUAL GIFTS LOOK LIKE FOR YOU?

Jumpstart Mentoring 8

"The Equipping"

Checking In:

You and your mentor should have lots to talk about today. This Session may have validated gifts you already know you have and gifts you are already using. This Session may have introduced some new things to you. I pray you and your Mentor have a great conversation about the type of person you are and what God may have gifted you to do. Remember, this is a journey. As you serve in the church and explore different areas of ministry I believe you will find your place of joy and effectiveness. Keep looking until you find it.

Conversation Starters:

1. Continue to study your way through each Session. Mark the things that interest and speak to you. Focus on what connects with your current walk. Go back through the lesson and share the verses and thoughts that touched you, challenged you, or bothered you.

_____

_____

_____

_____

Remember:

Studying the Bible is like eating a fish. Enjoy the meat and spit out the bones. Grab hold of the things you understand. If there are things you do not understand, do not worry, just keep studying. You will be surprised how things you learn in one area, will connect, and clarify things you read or study in another. The more you grow the more things will come together, and the whole will come into clearer focus. It's a lifetime of discovery.

2. Go back to the list of spiritual gifts.

A. Are you mostly a talker or a server? Is this consistent with your personality?

_____

_____

_____

B.   As you read the list of gifts, did you recognize some of them as things you already like to do?

_____

_____

_____

C.   Did you see a gift or calling you wish you had? Be willing to ask God.

_____

_____

_____

3.   Is there an area of service or ministry you would like to try? If there is talk to your Mentor, Shepherd, Coach, or Pastor. I expect they will love helping you discover the joy of serving according to your gifting.

_____

_____

Thought:

Do not allow spiritual gifts, especially the debate over tongues, to scare you off. Do not "Throw out the baby with the bathwater!" If you have questions that go beyond your mentoring grab your Shepherd, Coach, or Pastor.

There are excellent books and studies to help you discern the gifts God has given you. These are an excellent follow-up to JumpStart. Talk with your Mentor about this possibility. Nothing will ever replace the good old-fashioned process of trying ministries which look interesting to you. Invite people you trust to be honest with you about how well you do at that particular ministry. Another great method of discernment is to simply ask, "Am I having fun." When I am serving in my "sweet spot" it tends to produce joy, both for myself and for those I am serving.

If you are not enjoying it. And others are not enjoying it. Try something else. Do not suffer silently in a ministry you do not like. Sadly, that is how believers can become bitter. Life is too short, and the Body of Christ is too diverse, for you to stay stuck. Be honest with your leaders and try something else. Do this until you find the ministry where you fit. Then enjoy yourself and bless others.

OIKOS:

Last week you may have been asking, "How am I supposed to love and serve my OIKOS? How am I supposed to serve in the church?" This week you learned about the amazing gifts, talents, and abilities God has given you. You do not need to love, serve, and pray for your OIKOS by yourself. God has given you His Holy Spirit. He has given you supernatural abilities. He is at work in you and in your circle of influence. As you walk closely with Christ you will be amazed by the ways His life will organically flow through you to those around you. You do not need to force anything. Just love Jesus and allow Him to work through you. You will discover more about this in Volume Two.

Closing Suggestion:
Do you know what your spiritual gift is
and are you actively using it to God's glory?

A.   Work through the list of gifts.
B.   Go through the Talking and Serving categories.
C.   Consider your personality. Who are you really?
D.   What would you like to do? What would you like to try doing?
E.   What do Godly friends you trust see you doing?

MISSIONAL THOUGHT:

The awesome thing about gifts and personality is the amazing diversity in the Body of Christ. Doug was an Army Chaplain. Steve runs a camp. Justin is an Emergency Room Doctor. Pooh Bear was a police officer. Darla, Traci, and Teri are teachers or college professors. Mike runs a mission. Bud had prostitutes and Vegas showgirls in a Bible study he taught. He was their friend and they loved and trusted him. So did his wife! Walt is an overseas missionary. Next month Michael will be imbedded with a civilian chaplain assigned to a front line Ukrainian Army unit. Jennifer is a home school mom building a Lu La Roe business who can mesmerize hundreds of children with her Bible teaching. Chris pastors a church, runs a business, and rock climbs with his older children. Shannon helps lead a children's ministry and Jeremy can run a small group ministry for a church of several thousand people. They all do what they do to the glory of God, with joyful hearts. People see Christ in them every single day. All of it is awesome.

Other friends of mine washed dishes at Thousand Pines, served in soup kitchens, or passed out sandwiches to homeless people in Philadelphia. Each of these precious men and women are using their gifts to the glory of God. There is no pigeon hole or mold you must fit into. Do not allow someone else to stuff you into one.

My daughter went to a women's group once and was asked if she experienced limited opportunity in the Body of Christ growing up. She said no, "My dad always told me to do what God had gifted and called me to do." It's really just that simple. Do what you like to do. Do what you do well. Have fun serving Jesus anywhere! Be creative and out of the box. Go start a ministry nobody has ever thought of. Seek wise Christian counsel, and be deeply Biblical but don't ever let somebody lay the age old trip on you, "WE HAVE NEVER DONE IT THAT WAY BEFORE." Or, "YOU MIGHT FAIL." So what if you go down in flames! I have tried things in ministry that ended up being a waste of time and money. SO WHAT! LEARN FROM YOUR MISTAKES AND THEN GO TRY SOMETHING EVEN BIGGER AND CRAZIER. Blame it on me, I'm old enough to get away with stuff.

If you are reading this and fear has you by the throat, or if you are sitting their thinking, "I just can't do this, or I just can't try that, I'm too young, or I'm too old, or I'm a girl, or I'm a boy, or whatever." I want you to think of my dear sweet friend Roland.

In late 1999 Roland made an appointment to see me in my office. That was very formal and very unusual. He walked in and I asked him if anything was wrong. No, everything was fine. But he had found a younger woman and wanted to get married. He wanted me to do their counseling and the service. I laughed out loud about doing their pre-marital counseling. Waneta went to another church, but her pastor was a friend so I did not foresee a problem. On February 13th, 2000 I married them in the Fireside Room of our church. They honeymooned by train from California to New Jersey so he could show her where he was born and raised.

In March of 2015, two days before he died, I asked Roland his secret. He told me every night before he went to bed he got down on his knees and thanked Jesus for another day of life. I sat with him on his couch, to which he had walked. Tears rolled down my cheeks. We were holding hands, and I felt like I was touching a current that went straight to God. It was a holy moment. I asked Roland if he had any regrets. He thought a moment and then said to me, "Just one. My birthday is next month, and I don't think I will make it to 107."

**Find your gifts, unleash your passion, stop making excuses,
stop being afraid, take a big fat crazy chance,
and do something amazing with Jesus.**

Be Open:

You may be sitting in Life Group, Bible study, or worship and while somebody is sharing you get a clear insight from the Spirit about what needs to happen. Suddenly you know something or think something you have not seen, understood, or thought before.

Be open to how and when the Spirit may prompt you!
Do not be afraid. Be open. Trust God!
Follow His leading!
Do it kindly, wisely, and gently!

**You will never know how much God
wants to use you until you trust him enough
to allow Him to do so!**

VOLUME ONE BENEDICTION:

Lord God Almighty.
I receive Jesus Christ of Nazareth as my Lord and Savior.
I accept You as my Heavenly Father.
I invite the Holy Spirit to come into my life,
and be my teacher, guide, director, and comforter.

I submit my body, mind, soul, and resources to Christ
and His Kingdom. Lead me, guide me, direct me,
and protect me. I want to go where you want me to go,
say what you want me to say, do what you want me to do,
and be the man or woman of God you have called me to be.

Deliver me from the evil powers of this age.
Use me to your glory and receive me
into your eternal heavenly Kingdom when
my earthly journey in this world is finished.

In the mighty name of Jesus Christ,
AMEN

YOUR NEXT STEP

Congratulations on completing the first eight Sessions of JumpStart. You have invested many hours of study, prayer, and sharing. My prayer is you have grown in faith and knowledge. I pray this time birthed a deeper relationship with your Lord Jesus, Pastor, Mentor, Life Group, and local Church Fellowship.

If you are ready to take the next step you, your Mentor, or your group can proceed to JumpStart Volume Two.

JumpStart
Your Christian Discipleship

Volume One led you to study the basics of the Christian faith. Volume Two will explore Christ's call and how to put the call into practice. You will explore the powerful elements of Christian Stewardship. You will examine the Do's and Don'ts of Christian behavior. You will study the Character requirements for Christian leaders and what it looks like to live, lead, and serve in the Body of Christ. Finally, you will look at the Old and New Testament patterns of Celebration, Life Groups, and Mentoring. These represent large groups, small groups, and one on one relationships. No matter what words your local church uses to describe them, you will learn the Biblical foundations for them.

Volume One helped you learn the basics of Walking with Jesus. Volume Two will set you on the path to serving Him. I can't wait to see what He has for you! I would love an email about what God is doing in you, your group, or your church. If you found errors, or bad questions, I welcome your thoughts and corrections. JumpStart is always a work in progress.

My Prayer for You:

Lord, I pray for each and every person who has taken this time to study your Word and connect with a Mentor. I pray you fill them afresh with the power of your Holy Spirit. Help them grow and continue to learn. Form them into the man or woman of God you have called them to be. Break any chains them bind them, heal any memories that haunt them, and crush any habits that hinder them. Use them to your glory in the building of your Kingdom! In Jesus precious, mighty, amazing, and merciful name. AMEN

ABOUT THE AUTHOR:

Dr. Paul M. Reinhard was born at Ft. Sill, OK in 1955. His family soon returned to Southern California where he grew up and spent his youth. He graduated from Glendale High in 1973 and joined the U.S. Army on April 1, 1974. APRIL FOOLS!

He spent the next four years training and serving. He was on A-732 in Seventh Special Forces Group, and A-595 in Fifth Special Forces Group. Paul graduated from High Altitude Low Opening Parachute School (HALO) and Special Forces Under Water Operations (SFUWO). His team attended Jungle School in Panama, mountain operations in Puerto Rico, and Winter Warfare training in Alaska during January. During his last season of service his team worked and trained with a SADM (Strategic Atomic Demolition Munition.) This part of his training was only recently declassified by the U.S. Army.

While Paul held a Nuclear level security clearance by day he and his friends were devout "party animals" by night. In the summer of 1977 Paul's crazy lifestyle brought him to the point of decision. Through a multitude of "chance" encounters and events the Lord Jesus called Paul out of his sinful lifestyle and into the church.

In 1978 Paul was honorably discharged from the Army and returned to Glendale, CA. He met and married Karen Louise Maddux. He was attending L.I.F.E. Bible college when they learned Karen was pregnant with their first child. Paul needed a job so he applied, and was accepted, to the Glendale Police Department. Chris was born July 5, 1980 just days before Paul graduated from the Los Angeles Sheriff's Academy, Class 200.

While Glendale PD paid the bills Paul's heart and call where toward the ministry. Over the next few years Paul sold cars, ran a gardening route, and ultimately graduated from Azusa Pacific University with a B.A. in Biblical Literature. Daughter Jennifer was born July 20th, 1983 while Paul was still a student. He graduated in 1985.

The family began youth ministry at Sunland Baptist Church. Paul continued to study at Fuller Seminary. In 1988 the family moved to Fresno and Paul continued to study at California Theological Seminary by night. He worked at Power Burst as the Director of Special Events by day. In 1992 the family packed it up and moved to Woodstown, N.J. Paul was the part time Youth Pastor at First Baptist Church and a full time student at Eastern Baptist Theological Seminary, now Palmer Seminary. Paul graduated in 1994. In 1995 Paul accepted the call to Calvary Baptist Church in San Bernardino, CA where he pastored for twenty-one years.

Paul and Karen spent twenty-one years leading the church through a name change to NorthPoint, multimillion dollar arson fire, bankrupt insurance company, rebuild, and debt survival. They persisted in guiding a traditional Baptist church through changes in worship, constitution, and membership. Today the church is unified, growing, and pursuing God's will for her future under the excellent leadership of their son Chris!

In 2008 Paul began the Doctor of Ministry program at Golden Gate Theological Seminary, now Gateway. He had the privilege of being in the Cell Church cohort led by Dr. Ralph Neighbour, Jr. Over the past eight years God has tightened Paul's focus. Paul embraces large groups and loves Life Groups. However, he believes it is the one-on-one experience which transforms lives, shapes character, and prepares leaders.

Paul and Karen love doing life with their children Christopher and Jennifer, their spouses Shannon and Jeremy, and their six grandchildren Ashlee, Zoe, Hannah, Luke, Noah, and Busy Lizzy.

At sixty-one years of age Paul is feeling very blessed, alive, and curious about the next forty years! If Paul can serve you, your church, chapel, or ministry by speaking, dreaming, coaching, mentoring, or praying please reach out and connect.

CALL OR TEXT:
909-855-9695

EMAIL:
PaulMReinhard@Gmail.Com

PRAYERS AND NOTES:

PRAYERS AND NOTES:

PRAYERS AND NOTES:

59108737R00059

Made in the USA
Columbia, SC
04 June 2019